JN184351

English Insight

An Integrated Approach to Language Learning

Mark D. Stafford

Chizuko Tsumatori
Kozue Matsui

English Insight—An Integrated Approach to Language Learning

Mark D. Stafford
Chizuko Tsumatori / Kozue Matsui

© 2016 Cengage Learning K.K.

ALL RIGHTS RESERVED. No part of this work covered by the copyright herein may be reproduced, transmitted, stored, or used in any form or by any means—graphic, electronic, or mechanical, including but not limited to photocopying, recording, scanning, digitizing, taping, Web distribution, information networks, or information storage and retrieval systems—without the prior written permission of the publisher.

Photo Credits:
front cover: © Christopher Corr/Ikon Images; p. 7 © Thinkstock Images/Stockbyte/Thinkstock;
p. 11: © nito100/iStock/Thinkstock; p. 12: © Ingram Publishing/Thinkstock; p. 15: © Nastco/iStock/Thinkstock;
p. 20: © Rawpixel Ltd/iStock/Thinkstock; p. 23: © Fuse/Thinkstock; p. 28: © Creatas/Creatas/Thinkstock;
p. 31: © Creatas/Creatas/Thinkstock; p. 36: © Julia Grossi/Corbis; p. 39: © etorres69/iStock/Thinkstock;
p. 44: © ViktorCap/iStock/Thinkstock; p. 47: © Ron Chapple Stock/Ron Chapple Studios/Thinkstock;
p. 52: © yafoks/iStock/Thinkstock; p. 55: © J2R/iStock/Thinkstock; p. 59: © David Sacks/Photodisc/Thinkstock;
p. 60: © Jupiterimages/Polka Dot/Thinkstock; p. 83: © Wavebreakmedia Ltd/Wavebreak media/Thinkstock;
p. 68: © moodboard/moodboard/Thinkstock; p. 71: © Wavebreakmedia/iStock/Thinkstock;
p. 74: © BakiBG/iStock/Thinkstock; p. 76: © Rawpixel Ltd/iStock/Thinkstock; p. 79: © moodboard/moodboard/Thinkstock; p. 84: © fotokostic/iStock/Thinkstock; p. 87: © Image Source White/Image Source/Thinkstock;
p. 92: © PaulMaguire/iStock/Thinkstock; p. 95: © mihtiander/iStock/Thinkstock; p. 99: © extravagantni/iStock/Thinkstock; p. 100: © furtaev/iStock/Thinkstock; p. 103: © g-stockstudio/iStock/Thinkstock; p. 107: © Halfpoint/iStock/Thinkstock; p. 108: © Jupiterimages/Stockbyte/Thinkstock; p. 111: © Bee-individual/iStock Editorial/Thinkstock;
p. 116: © Noel Hendrickson/Photodisc/Thinkstock

For permission to use material from this textbook or product, e-mail to **elt@cengagejapan.com**

ISBN: 978-4-86312-280-2

Cengage Learning K.K.
No. 2 Funato Building 5th Floor
1-11-11 Kudankita, Chiyoda-ku
Tokyo 102-0073
Japan

Tel: 03-3511-4392
Fax: 03-3511-4391

Contents

4		Preface	
5		ユニットの基本構成	
Pages	Units	Titles	Grammar Points
7	Unit 1	From My Heart To Yours [贈り物]	代名詞
15	Unit 2	To Be Or Not To Be [国籍とアイデンティティ]	be 動詞
23	Unit 3	Too Many Calories? [食習慣]	名詞
31	Unit 4	Life With A Roommate [共同生活]	冠詞と限定詞
39	Unit 5	I'll Take A Vacation! [休暇]	一般動詞
47	Unit 6	How Is The Weather? [気候]	疑問文
55	Unit 7	Did You Do The Dishes? [家事]	過去時制
63	Unit 8	I'm Going To College [学生生活]	進行形
71	Unit 9	Have You Ever Had A Job? [就職活動]	現在完了
79	Unit 10	She Had Been Great! [表彰]	過去完了
87	Unit 11	How Is Christmas Celebrated? [クリスマス]	受動態
95	Unit 12	Do You Want To Take Some Time Off? [長期休暇の過ごし方]	不定詞
103	Unit 13	I Can Drive! [運転免許]	助動詞 can, will
111	Unit 14	Where Would You Like To Go? [ドライブ旅行]	助動詞 could, would
119		References	

Preface

English Insight is an innovative textbook designed to introduce (or reintroduce) students to basic aspects of English grammar in an interactive and motivating fashion. Although instructors may find interest and delight in the functions of English grammar, many students view learning grammar as a rather futile and discouraging endeavor. For them, it is similar to learning a sport by reading a manual but never experiencing its fun and exciting kinesthetic aspects. Yet, language also belongs to the physical world where users must utilize not only their brains, but also eyes, ears, mouth, facial expressions, and body gestures to exchange information.

English Insight intends to bridge such a divide between conceptual and practical aspects of English grammar education. As its title suggests, this book aims to give students *insight* into how features of English grammar function in real and practical situations. Students will become deeply engrossed in using the language while also learning its rules, and they will do so from the very first activity.

Aspects of conventional English grammar-learning activities have been included in this book. However, to help students gain greater insight into how grammar operates in real contexts, variations on such conventions were developed.

For example, learners must use conventional reasoning to complete gap-fill activities, but also employ more deductive thinking for proofreading and correcting exercises in some of the Grammar Insight and United Skills activities. Also, an innovative approach to vocabulary-learning, where students guess word meanings through context (a vital reading skill), was developed for the Word Power section. Furthermore, in the Listen Up! and Ready to Read? sections, students must complete passages with the unit's targeted grammar features and new vocabulary in addition to answering conventional comprehension questions.

Each of these multi-faceted activities not only makes language learning more interactive and, hopefully, interesting to students, but also fosters a more intimate relationship between them and the learning materials. Additionally, unit themes were chosen not only for their suitability to the targeted grammar features, but also for cultural content of high interest for young people—students often learn about foreign customs compared to their own culture through a young person's perspective. Moreover, students can personalize activities in the Write to Speak and United Skills sections by adding their own information, making them even more interactive and motivating.

Although still conventional in some aspects, English Insight has taken large strides in making grammar-based language learning more interactive, motivating, and... *insightful*!

Mark D. Stafford

本書では、文法事項や語彙を"読んで書き、聞いて話す"という4技能すべてを通して繰り返し使えるように工夫されています。このことにより、文法や語彙をより理解しやすく覚えやすくなるでしょう。また各ユニットでは、北米の学生たちの生活を垣間見ることができるトピックを扱っています。「バレンタインデー」「夏休み」「就職活動」など、皆さんにとって身近なものばかりです。自分たちの生活や考え方と比較してみることで、自分たち自身の文化との違いを深く理解できるでしょう。このように活用していただけたら、本書作成に携わった者として光栄です。

妻鳥千鶴子、松井こずえ

ユニットの基本構成

Grammar Insight

ユニットで扱う文法ポイントの基本知識を身につけます。そのポイントを自分で実際に使いながら解く練習問題やアクティビティで構成されています。ユニット全体で「読み、書き、聞き、そして話す」という4技能を通じて、文法ポイントを繰り返し練習するようになっているので、より理解度を深め、自分のものにしやすくなるでしょう。

Write to Speak

学習した文法ポイントを使いながら、筋が通るように会話文を完成させます。自分のことを答えるようになっている部分もあります。完成させたら、パートナーと一緒にその会話を練習します。単に読み上げるのではなく、できるだけ表現や文を覚えてから言うと、さらに効果があります。

Word Power

ユニットのトピックと関連のある語彙を学びます。文中に使われた別の表現部分を学習ターゲットの語彙で置き換えます。最初は難しく思えるかもしれませんが、単に空所を補充することとは異なり、より語彙について深く理解でき、覚えやすくなるでしょう。また、文中における語彙を推測するという読解力アップに必要不可欠な練習にもなります。

Listen Up!

ユニットの文法ポイントを盛り込んだダイアログを聞きます。最初は何も見ないで聞いて質問に答えることが、リスニング力の向上につながります。また、学習した語彙と文法ポイントで空所を補充してダイアログを完成させるアクティビティも用意し、リスニングを通した語彙と文法の定着を目指します。

Ready to Read?

ユニットのテーマについて書き下ろした、学生にとって面白く関連性の深い本文のリーディングです。まずは文法ポイントと語彙の練習を行うため、空所補充で文章を完成させます。読後は True/False の問題で全体の内容理解度を測り、次に細部に関する問題を解いて、文章の理解を深めます。

United Skills

最後に学んだ語彙と文法ポイントを総動員させます。最初の文章を訂正するアクティビティでは、「読む・聞く」ことを同時に行いつつ、知識の整理を行うことができます。次に質問が提示されているので、自分自身の回答を書き、それをパートナーに話すというアクティビティを行うことでスピーキングの練習もできます。

音声ファイルの無料ダウンロード

http://cengage.jp/elt/JapaneseFourSkills/

🎧 のアイコンがある箇所の音声ファイルをダウンロードできます。

❶ 上記 URL にアクセスまたは QR コードをスマートフォンなどのリーダーでスキャン（→❹へ）
❷ 本書の表紙画像またはタイトル（English Insight）をクリック
❸ 本書のページで 音声ファイル ボタンをクリック
❹ 希望の番号をクリックして音声ファイルをダウンロード

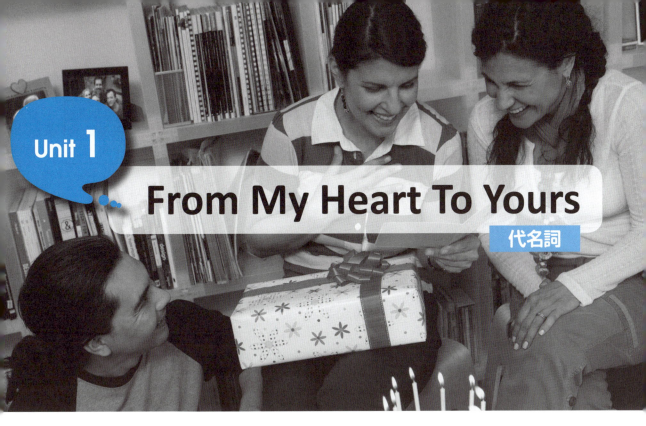

Unit 1
From My Heart To Yours
代名詞

Grammar Insight

主格の代名詞：文の主語になり、日本語の「〜は、〜が」にあたります。

単数			複数		
一人称	二人称	三人称	一人称	二人称	三人称
I	you	he, she, it	we	you	they

A 例にならい、（　）内の語句を代名詞に変えて空所に入れ、英文を完成させましょう。

例 Her home is Hong Kong, so *she* is Chinese. (Lin)

1. _____ like playing sports. (my friends and I)
2. _____ are university students. (Thomas and Julie)
3. _____ says hi to you. (Ken)
4. Can _____ join us for dinner? (you and Patrick)
5. Nancy has two children, doesn't _____? (Nancy)

所有格の代名詞：日本語の「〜の」にあたり、後ろに名詞が続きます。

単数			複数		
一人称	二人称	三人称	一人称	二人称	三人称
my	your	his, her, its	our	your	their

B 例にならい、（　）内の日本語に合う代名詞を空所に入れ、英文を完成させましょう。

例　These are not *his* books. (彼の)

1. I'd like to introduce _____ friend, Dan. (私の)
2. _____ hard work will pay off. (あなたの)
3. _____ office is on the third floor. (私たちの)
4. These are _____ rooms. (彼らの)
5. The company advertised _____ new brand. (その)

目的格の代名詞：動詞の目的語になったり、前置詞の後ろに続いたりします。日本語の「〜を、〜に」にあたります。

単数			複数		
一人称	二人称	三人称	一人称	二人称	三人称
me	you	him, her, it	us	you	them

所有代名詞：日本語の「〜のもの」にあたり、主語や目的語になります。

単数			複数		
一人称	二人称	三人称	一人称	二人称	三人称
mine	yours	his, hers	ours	yours	theirs

C 例にならい、（　）内の日本語に合う代名詞を空所に入れ、英文を完成させましょう。

例　Give it to *me*. (私に)

1. This book is _____, isn't it? (私のもの)
2. She told _____ to stay here. (私たちに)
3. Sarah gave _____ a watch. (彼に)
4. My bicycle is old, but _____ are new. (彼らのもの)
5. I gave the teacher my paper, but she still needs _____. (あなたのもの)

UNIT 1 From My Heart To Yours

Write to Speak

▶ 例にならい、（ ）内の日本語訳に合うように、空所に適切な代名詞を入れ、会話を完成させましょう。完成後、パートナーと会話練習をしましょう。

例 A: Are you wearing _my_ shoes?（私の靴を履いているの？）
　　B: No. They are _mine_.（いいえ、私［自分］のものよ）

1. A: I met a friend of _____.（君の友達に会ったよ）
   B: Who was that?（それって誰？）

2. A: Is this _____ pen, or Ken's?（これは君のペン？それともケンの？）
   B: That's _____.（それは私のよ）

3. A: What did _____ say to _____?（彼はあなたに何と言ったの？）
   B: _____ parents are coming tomorrow.（彼の両親が明日来るって）

4. A: Did Paul give a present to Mayumi?（ポールはマユミにプレゼントをあげたの？）
   B: Yes, _____ gave _____ a laptop computer.
   （うん、彼は彼女にノートパソコンをね）

5. A: Would _____ like to join _____ for lunch?
   （僕らと一緒にお昼を食べない？）
   B: Sounds great!（いいね）

Word Power

▶ 例にならい、英文中の太字で示した部分を枠内の語句で書き換えましょう。

- ☑ celebrate
- ☐ coworker
- ☐ expensive
- ☐ greeting cards
- ☐ jewelry
- ☐ romantic
- ☐ tradition
- ☐ watch

例 Let's **enjoy** Christmas together this year.
　　　celebrate

1. Ken wears a **clock on his arm** every day.

2. A diamond ring is a very **high cost** present.

3. Paris is a city that is very **full of love**.

4. Americans usually get **message papers** on their birthdays.

5. Jan bought Amy some **gold and diamond accessories** for her birthday.

6. Stan's **person who works together** is only 20 years old.

7. Taking off your shoes when you go into a house is a Japanese **something people usually do**.

Listen Up!

 **A** 会話を聞いて、問いに対する適切な解答を丸で囲みましょう。

1. Is Patrick's birthday soon? — [Yes, it is. / No, it isn't.]
2. Does Nancy know what Patrick wants? — [Yes, she does. / No, she doesn't.]
3. Will Sam and Nancy buy a gift together? — [Yes, they will. / No, they won't.]
4. Does Patrick like Sam's and Nancy's watches? — [Yes, he does. / No, he doesn't.]

UNIT 1 From My Heart To Yours

5. What will Sam and Nancy give Patrick? — [A greeting card. / A watch.]
6. Will Sam and Nancy go to a clothing store? — [Yes, they will. / No, they won't.]

B 空所に枠内の単語を適切な形で入れて、会話を完成させましょう。

☐ expensive	☐ gift	☐ he	☐ him	☐ his
☐ jewelry	☐ me	☐ mine	☐ nice	☐ one
☐ ours	☐ us	☐ you	☐ watch	

Sam: Nancy, what will you give Patrick for ¹._____ birthday?

Nancy: I'm not sure. I don't know what ²._____ wants. How about ³._____, Sam?

Sam: I want to buy ⁴._____ something a little ⁵._____ this year.

Nancy: Hey! Let's give him a ⁶._____ ⁷._____ together!

Sam: That's a great idea! Let's see… He said he likes my ⁸._____.

Nancy: He said he likes ⁹._____, too.

Sam: Well, he likes watches, so let's buy him a really nice one.

Nancy: Sounds good to ¹⁰._____. That will be a great present.

Sam: Where can we buy ¹¹._____?

Nancy: Let's go to the ¹²._____ store together.

Sam: All right. I really hope he likes the present from ¹³._____!

Nancy: ¹⁴._____ will be the best!

C 音声を聞いて **B** の答えを確認しましょう。また、パートナーと **B** の会話を読み合いましょう。

Ready to Read?

A 空所に枠内の語句を入れて、文章を完成させましょう。

- celebrate
- coworkers
- greeting card
- him
- his
- mine
- my
- nice
- romantic
- she
- their
- them
- they
- tradition
- us

Valentine's Day Traditions 🎧 03

People in many countries ¹._____ Valentine's Day, but the way they celebrate is often very different in each place. You probably know about the *girichoko* (義理チョコ) ². _____ in Japan where women give chocolate to their male ³._____ and friends. But do you know that North Americans celebrate

5 Valentine's Day in three very different ways?

Of course ⁴._____ celebrate ⁵._____ love with someone special. A boyfriend or husband will often give a ⁶._____, chocolate, and flowers to ⁷._____ girlfriend or wife and ⁸._____ will give ⁹._____ a greeting card, chocolate,

10 and maybe a gift. They may also have a ¹⁰._____, romantic dinner together.

North Americans also often celebrate family love on Valentine's Day. Our mothers and fathers give ¹¹._____ a greeting card and chocolate on

15 February 14th and we give ¹²._____ the same. Greeting cards I received help me remember my family's love, so I always put ¹³._____ on my desk.

12

UNIT 1　From My Heart To Yours

Another type of love that is celebrated in North America is friendship. Many school children give greeting cards to ¹⁴·_____ classmates on Valentine's Day. But most schools have a special rule that students must give a greeting card to all of their classmates. I followed the rule, but I always gave the best card to ¹⁵·_____ favorite girl.

People usually think that Valentine's Day is a celebration of romantic love. But it is also a celebration of family love and friendship in North America.

NOTES　way「方法」　male「男性の」　another「もう１つの」　special rule「特別な規則」
　　　　follow「…に従う」　favorite「好きな」　celebration「お祝い」

B 次の英文が **A** の文章と合っていれば True を、合っていなければ False を丸で囲みましょう。

1. People celebrate Valentine's Day the same way around the world.　　[True / False]
2. *Girichoko* (義理チョコ) is also a tradition in North America.　　[True / False]
3. Three types of love are celebrated in North America.　　[True / False]

C **A** の文章に関する質問の答えとして、最も適切なものを選びましょう。

1. What might a North American girl give her boyfriend for Valentine's Day?
   (A) Flowers
   (B) Nothing
   (C) A present

2. What do North American children give their parents for Valentine's Day?
   (A) A greeting card and chocolate
   (B) Flowers and chocolate
   (C) A book and greeting card

3. Who did the writer always give the best greeting card to?
   (A) His wife
   (B) His mother and father
   (C) His favorite girl

United Skills

 A 音声を聞きながら、次の文章を読みましょう。音声と異なる個所があるので、丸で囲みましょう（10個所）。

My wonderful grandmother said that hers 90th birthday was the best of her life. All of her grandchildren came to see it that day. We love him so much, so we gave him expensive gifts, beautiful flowers, and a nice birthday cake. He invited we to come again for your 100th birthday! They all said that me would try ours best!

 B もう一度音声を聞いて、丸で囲んだ個所を訂正しましょう。

C 次の質問に対し、自分の答えを英語で書きましょう。

1. How do you usually celebrate the birthdays of your family members and friends?
   （家族や友達の誕生日を普段どのように祝いますか）

   _____
   _____

2. What do you want for your birthday or Valentine's Day?
   （誕生日やバレンタインデーに欲しいプレゼントは何ですか）

   _____
   _____

D パートナーと交互に、**C** の質問と答えの発話練習をしましょう。

Unit 2
To Be Or Not To Be
be 動詞

Grammar Insight

be 動詞の肯定形

主語	be 動詞	例文
I	**am**	I **am** [I'**m**] Canadian.
he / she / it	**is**	He **is** [He'**s**] in Chicago.
we / you / they	**are**	We **are** [We'**re**] going to Toronto.

A 例にならい、（ ）内の語句と be 動詞を空所に入れて、英文を完成させましょう。

例 <u>You are</u> much taller than me. (You)

1. _____ _____ very fun to do with friends. (Singing)
2. _____ _____ going to Las Vegas tomorrow. (I)
3. _____ _____ _____ _____ from the United States of America. (Carl and Sandy)
4. _____ _____ _____ smaller than last year. (The group)
5. _____ _____ in San Francisco now. (We)

be 動詞の否定形

主語	be 動詞	例文
I	**am** *not*	I'**m** *not* the manager.
he / she / it	**is** *not*	She **is** *not* [**isn't**] working today.
we / you / they	**are** *not*	You **are** *not* [**aren't**] going to a movie.

B 例にならい、肯定文を否定文に直しましょう。

例 They ~~are~~ eating dinner now.
    aren't

1. She's living in a big apartment.

2. I'm interested in American music.

3. It's so hot these days.

4. You are so late for work.

5. We are happy about the new rules.

be 動詞を使った Yes/No 疑問文

be 動詞	主語	例文
am	I	**Am** I next?
is	he / she / it	**Is** it working now?
are	we / you / they	**Are** they eating dinner late?

be 動詞を使った wh 疑問文

Wh 疑問詞	be 動詞	主語	例文
why / when / where	am	I	*Why* **am** I last?
	is	he / she / it	*When* **is** he coming home?
	are	we / you / they	*Where* **are** you going on vacation?

C 例にならい、（ ）内の語句と be 動詞を空所に入れて、英文を完成させましょう。

例 *Are you* cooking dinner now? (you)

1. What _____ _____ going to see? (I)
2. How _____ _____ _____ _____ going home? (Ken and Amy)
3. _____ _____ _____ going to call you later? (Mr. Wilson)
4. Why _____ _____ _____ so sad today? (Ms. Holmes)
5. _____ _____ going with you? (I)

Write to Speak

▶ 例にならい、空所に適する語句を入れ、会話を完成させましょう。B は自分のことを答えましょう。完成後、パートナーと会話練習をしましょう。

例 A: How *is* your friend?
　　B: He/She *is* very fine every day!

1. A: _____ I taller than you?
   B: Yes, _____ _____. / No, _____ _____.

2. A: Who _____ your favorite actors?
   B: _____ _____ _____ and _____.

3. A: _____ this class in a high school?
   B: Yes, _____ _____. / No, _____ _____.

4. A: _____ _____ from Hawaii?
   B: No, _____ _____. _____ from _____.

5. A: What _____ you doing now?
   B: _____ speaking to you of course!

Word Power

▶ 例にならい、英文中の太字で示した部分を枠内の語句で書き換えましょう。必要があれば、適切な形にしましょう。

☐ ancestors	☐ be born	☐ be interested in	☐ birthplace
☐ citizen	☐ identity	☑ immigrate	☐ nationality

例 Rolf will **change his country** to Canada from Germany.
　　　　　immigrate

1. My sister's baby will **join the world** next month.

2. Anna changed her **country that she belongs to** two years ago.

3. Anna is now a Canadian **person**.

4. My **first town** is Portland in Oregon.

5. Ken **wants to know about** Kim's trip to Korea.

6. My **family members a long time ago** were from northern Europe.

7. Karen feels that her **own character** is more French than Canadian.

Listen Up!

🎧 05 **A** 会話を聞いて、次の表を完成させましょう。

	Birthplace	Citizen of	Now living in
Amy			
Carlos			

🎧 05 **B** もう一度会話を聞いて、問いに対する適切な解答を丸で囲みましょう。

1. Was Amy born in America? — [Yes, she was. / No, she wasn't.]

2. Is Amy an American citizen? — [Yes, she is. / No, she isn't.]
3. Was Carlos born in America? — [Yes, he was. / No, he wasn't.]
4. Is Carlos an American citizen? — [Yes, he is. / No, he isn't.]
5. Where are Carlos and Amy living now? — They're living in [America / Mexico].
6. What are Carlos' and Amy's nationalities? — They're both [American / Mexican].

C 空所に枠内の語句を適切な形で入れて、会話を完成させましょう。2回以上使うものもあります。

☐ are	☐ birthplace	☐ born	☐ citizen
☐ I'm	☐ immigrate	☐ interested	☐ is
☐ nationality	☐ we're	☐ you're	

Amy: Hi Carlos. How ¹._____ you today?

Carlos: ²._____ fine. How about you?

Amy: Me too. Hey, can I ask you something about your ³._____?

Carlos: Sure. What do you want to know?

Amy: Well, I was ⁴._____ in America, and I have lived here all my life.

Carlos: Yes, I know. ⁵._____ an American ⁶._____, right?

Amy: Sure. But, ⁷._____ ⁸._____ to know about you. I heard ⁹._____ from Mexico.

Carlos: That's right. My ¹⁰._____ ¹¹._____ Mexico but my family ¹²._____ to America 15 years ago.

Amy: Oh, I see. So, ¹³._____ you a Mexican or American citizen now?

Carlos: My parents, my sister, and I ¹⁴._____ all American citizens now.

Amy: Hey, just like me!

Carlos: Yes, ¹⁵._____ both Americans.

D 音声を聞いて **C** の答えを確認しましょう。また、パートナーと **C** の会話を読み合いましょう。

Ready to Read?

A 空所に枠内の単語を入れて、文章を完成させましょう。2回以上使うものもあります。

- am
- ancestors
- are
- identity
- is
- nationality

Nationality & Identity

What ¹._____ your nationality? How about your identity? If you are from a country like Japan, this might be easy for you to answer. For many people, nationality and identity ²._____ the same. But nationality and identity are not so clear in other countries like the U.S.A.

My ³._____ came to the United States from England, Holland, Scotland, and Spain many years ago. They were English, Dutch, Scottish, and Spanish. But my family has lived in the U.S.A. for so many years that I don't feel like I ⁴._____ any of these nationalities. Instead, my ⁵._____ is simply American.

I have some friends who were born in the U.S.A. but their parents ⁶._____ from Mexico. Their ⁷._____ is American and they hold American passports but their identities ⁸._____ very much Mexican. Even though they are from the U.S.A., they speak Spanish, eat Mexican food, and celebrate Mexican holidays.

I have another friend who recently changed his nationality from Brazilian to American. He likes Brazil very much but he thought it ⁹·_____ better to be American because his children prefer to live in the U.S.A. When I asked him if he feels Brazilian or American, he said his identity is about 70-percent Brazilian and 30-percent American.

After all, your nationality depends on the country that gives you your passport, but your identity ¹⁰·_____ in your heart.

NOTES Holland「オランダ」 Dutch「オランダ人」 instead「代わりに」 hold「持っている」 recently「最近」 prefer to *do*「…することのほうを好む」 after all「結局」 depend on「…次第である」

B 次の英文が **A** の文章と合っていれば True を、合っていなければ False を丸で囲みましょう。

1. Nationality and identity are always the same in the U.S.A. 　　[True / False]
2. Your nationality always depends on the country of your passport. 　　[True / False]
3. Your identity depends on how you feel. 　　[True / False]

C **A** の文章に関する質問の答えとして、最も適切なものを選びましょう。

1. Which identity does the writer feel most?
    (A) English
    (B) Spanish
    (C) American

2. Where were the writer's Mexican-American friends born?
    (A) Mexico
    (B) America
    (C) Spain

3. What did the writer's Brazilian friend say about his identity?
    (A) He feels more Brazilian than American.
    (B) He feels more American than Brazilian.
    (C) He feels equally Brazilian and American.

United Skills

 A 音声を聞きながら、次の文章を読みましょう。音声と異なる個所があるので、丸で囲みましょう（10個所）。

My parents is both European. My mother am from Portugal and my father are from Spain. They have lived in Canada for 20 years and is Canadian citizens now. But, I are not European. My ancestors is all European, but my nationality am Canadian. Sometimes people ask me, "What are your nationality?" I always tell them that I is Canadian, but my family are from Europe.

 B もう一度音声を聞いて、丸で囲んだ個所を訂正しましょう。

C 次の質問に対し、自分の答えを英語で書きましょう。

1. When do you think about your nationality or identity?
   （いつ自分の国籍やアイデンティティーについて考えることがありますか）

2. If you could change your nationality, which one would you like? Why?
   （国籍を変えることができるとすれば、どれがよいですか。その理由は何ですか）

D パートナーと交互に、**C**の質問と答えの発話練習をしましょう。

Unit 3 Too Many Calories?

名詞

Grammar Insight

名詞の複数形

複数形が規則的に変化する名詞 （語尾に -s または -es を付ける）		複数形が不規則に変化する名詞		複数形が変化しない名詞
単数形	複数形	単数形	複数形	単複同形
book	book**s**	mouse	m**ice**	fish
tax	tax**es**	woman	wom**en**	sheep
table	table**s**	foot	f**ee**t	yen

A 枠内の名詞が属するグループを考え、上の表に書き込みましょう。

box   child   dog   life   percent   salmon   series

B 例にならい、太字で示した名詞を必要があれば複数形に変えましょう。

例 We need five **apple** to bake this pie.
　　　　　apples

1. Two **man** are waiting in your office.

2. The best **peach** come from Georgia.

3. Donna saw many **deer** in the forest, but she didn't see any **snake**.

4. Albert broke three **tooth** when he fell down.

5. Twenty **person** came to the meeting.

不可算名詞（物質的なもの）

液体	気体	小片	塊	s が付かない 集合的なもの	s が付く 集合的なもの
water	smoke	rice	ice	money	clothes
tea	oxygen	salt	cheese	mail	supplies
milk	gas	sugar	gold	work	

C 枠内の名詞が属するグループを考え、上の表に書き込みましょう。

air	bread	fireworks	gasoline	goods
homework	jewelry	juice	meat	
popcorn	sand	stairs	steam	

不可算名詞（抽象的なもの）

性質・概念	自然現象	言語	学問	運動競技・動作
music	rain	English	art	reading
beauty	space	grammar	law	soccer
happiness	fire	slang	math	dance

D 枠内の名詞が属するグループを考え、上の表に書き込みましょう。

chemistry	driving	French	light	luck
peace	science	swimming	vocabulary	weather

Write to Speak

▶ 例にならい、太字で示した名詞を必要があれば複数形に変え、また空所に適する語句を入れ、会話を完成させましょう。B は自分のことを答えましょう。完成後、パートナーと会話練習をしましょう。

例 A: Do you have any **pet**?
　　　　　　　　　　　pets
　　B: [(Yes, I have) / No, I don't have] *a pet / pets*.

1. A: Do you prefer **meat** or **vegetable**?

   B: I prefer ＿＿＿＿＿＿＿＿.

2. A: How often do you brush your **tooth**?

   B: I brush my ＿＿＿＿＿＿ ＿＿＿＿＿＿ time(s) every day.

3. A: Do you drink tea with or without **sugar**?

   B: I have my tea [with / without] ＿＿＿＿＿＿＿.

4. A: Do you like **swimming**?

   B: [Yes, I do / No, I don't] like ＿＿＿＿＿＿＿.

5. A: What are your two favorite **animal**?

   B: I like ＿＿＿＿＿＿ and ＿＿＿＿＿＿ most.

 Word Power

▶ 例にならい、英文中の太字で示した部分を枠内の語句で書き換えましょう。

☐ people   ☐ person   ☐ pie   ☐ pound
☐ pumpkin ☐ size   ☑ turkey

例 Americans eat **a bigger bird than a chicken** much more than Japanese do.
　　　　　　　　　　　　　turkey

1. I love to eat **a kind of sweet food** for dessert.

2. Sandy thinks there are too many **humans** in New York City.

3. Pie is often made of **a kind of big, round vegetable** in North America.

4. One **Brisith and North American weight measurement** is the same as 0.45 kilograms.

5. There is one **human** waiting in the lobby.

6. My shoe **number of how big** is 27.

 Listen Up!

A 会話を聞いて、問いに対する適切な解答を丸で囲みましょう。

1. Are Leslie and Brian talking about a birthday? — [Yes, they are. / No, they aren't.]
2. What will Leslie and Brian do together? — [Buy presents. / Cook dinner.]
3. How many people will they invite? — [16. / 18.]
4. How many turkeys will they buy? — [One. / Two.]
5. What kind of sauce will they buy? — [Cranberry. / Butter.]
6. What will they bake for dessert? — [A Christmas cake. / A pumpkin pie.]

UNIT 3 Too Many Calories?

B 音声を聞き、空所に枠内の名詞を適切な形で入れて、会話を完成させましょう。

☐ bird	☐ bread	☐ butter	☐ family	☐ member
☐ people	☐ person	☐ pie	☐ potato	☐ pound
☐ pumpkin	☐ sauce	☐ size	☐ sugar	☐ turkey

Leslie: Brian, what should we cook for Christmas?

Brian: Well, Leslie. How about having a traditional Christmas dinner with 1._____?

Leslie: Sounds good to me. What 2._____ should we buy?

Brian: Let's see… It's best to buy one 3._____ for each 4._____.

Leslie: All right. So, how many people will we invite?

Brian: Well, everybody in your 5._____ and about seven of my family 6._____.

Leslie: OK. Let's invite 16 7._____. Wow! Including us, we need to buy 18 pounds of turkey.

Brian: I don't think we can find such a big one.

Leslie: Then, how about cooking two smaller 8._____?

Brian: That's a good idea.

Leslie: We also have to buy lots of 9._____, some 10._____, and some cranberry 11._____.

Brian: Don't forget 12._____, 13._____, and a 14._____ so we can bake a 15._____!

C パートナーと B の会話を読み合いましょう。

27

Ready to Read?

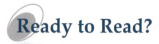 必要があれば、太字の名詞を複数形に変えましょう。

Counting Calories

How many times do you eat fast ¹·**food** every week? Once? Twice? Three times? Well, it's probably less than a typical American who has hamburgers, French fries, ²·**cola**, and other ³·**type** of fast food about 5.8 ⁴·**time** a week.

It may be surprising to you that one out of four Americans eat some type of fast food every day. In fact, the U.S. ⁵·**government** found that the average American ate nearly 2,000 ⁶·**pound** or 907 ⁷·**kilogram** of food each ⁸·**year**. The government also found that 11.3 percent of this food comes from fast food ⁹·**restaurant**. This means that an average American eats about 103 kilograms of fast food every year.

Americans spend a lot of ¹⁰·**money** on this fast food. Researchers found that after paying ¹¹·**tax**, they spend 10 percent of their extra money on fast food every year. This means Americans spend more than 110 billion U.S. ¹²·**dollar** or 13,200,000,000,000 Japanese ¹³·**yen** on fast food!

Of course, eating all of this fast food is not good for our ¹⁴·**health**. Nearly 70 percent of ¹⁵·**adult** and more than 30 percent of American ¹⁶·**child** are overweight. Being

overweight causes many dangerous diseases. However, Americans are starting to change their bad eating habits by eating less fast food. They are also eating more low-fat [17.] **chicken** than high-fat [18.] **beef** for the first time in 100 [19.] **year**.

Fast food certainly tastes good, but, like many things in [20.] **life**, it's best to control how much you have.

NOTES French fries「フライドポテト」 in fact「実際に」 average「平均的な」 researcher「研究者」
overweight「太り過ぎの」 disease「病気」 habit「習慣」 low-/high-fat「低／高脂肪の」

B 次の英文が **A** の文章と合っていれば True を、合っていなければ False を丸で囲みましょう。

1. A typical American eats a lot of fast food. [True / False]
2. Americans don't spend a lot of their extra money on fast food. [True / False]
3. Americans are changing their fast food habits. [True / False]

C **A** の文章に関する質問の答えとして、最も適切なものを選びましょう。

1. How much fast food does a typical American eat each year?
    (A) 2,000 pounds
    (B) 103 kilograms
    (C) 907 kilograms

2. How much of their extra money do Americans spend on fast food every year?
    (A) 11.3%
    (B) 10%
    (C) 30%

3. What do Americans eat more of recently?
    (A) Chicken
    (B) Beef
    (C) Fast food

United Skills

A 音声を聞きながら、次の文章を読みましょう。音声と異なる個所があるので、丸で囲みましょう（10個所）。

I'm a typical university students, so I usually don't eat healthy foods. I'm so busy going to many class and studying that I don't want to cook anything in a hot kitchens. I usually eat fast food like hamburger or sandwich on my way home from schools. My mother says I need to eat more fishes and vegetable, and drink fruit juices instead of cola.

B もう一度音声を聞いて、丸で囲んだ個所を訂正しましょう。

C 次の質問に対し、自分の答えを英語で書きましょう。

1. How often do you eat fast food?　（どれくらいの頻度でファストフードを食べますか）

   _____
   _____

2. What kind of food do you like?　（どんな食べ物が好きですか）

   _____
   _____

D パートナーと交互に、**C** の質問と答えの発話練習をしましょう。

Unit 4 — Life With A Roommate

冠詞と限定詞

Grammar Insight

不定冠詞：a や母音の前にくる an のことで、どちらも単数の名詞の前に付けます。

a	an
He met **a** friend. I read **a** book. They live in **a** big city.	She is **an** engineer. I ate **an** apple. We saw **an** interesting movie.

◎**不定冠詞を付けない場合**：複数や不可算の名詞

　She writes **books**. ／ Do you like **music**? ／ We ate **bread** with **butter**.

定冠詞：the のことで、基本的な用法は次の2つです。単数と複数、どちらの名詞にも付けます。

① **同じ名詞を繰り返す場合**：最初は a を使い、次から the を使います。

　I live in **a** house. **The** house is very small.
　She baked **a** cake, then she ate **the** cake.

② **世間一般で共通に認識している場合**

　He is **the** president of **the** United States.
　I looked at **the** sun, **the** moon, and **the** stars.

31

◎**定冠詞を付けない場合**：地名
They live in **Florida**.
He climbed **Mount Everest**.
Lake Titicaca is in **Peru** and **Bolivia**.

A 例にならい、[ ]内の適切なものを丸で囲み、英文を完成させましょう。冠詞を入れる必要がない場合は×を選びましょう。

例 I gave [(a) / an / ×] pen to my friend.

1. He cooked [a / an / ×] egg.
2. What kind of [an / the / ×] animals do you like?
3. I have [a / an / ×] cat and [a / the / ×] cat is so cute.
4. Are you interested in climbing [an / the / ×] Mount Fuji?
5. Bob and Susan looked at [an / the / ×] big blue sky.

指示詞：this や that などのことです。名詞の前に付けます。

単数		複数	
this	that	these	those
This room is mine.	**That** bag over there is yours.	**These** books are mine.	**Those** pens are yours.

B 例にならい、空所に指示詞を入れて、英文を完成させましょう。単数と複数に注意しましょう。

例 Is *this* bag on my desk yours?

1. I think _____ keys here in my bag are yours.
2. _____ people across the street are my friends.
3. Let's meet at _____ bus stop 50 meters away from here.
4. _____ drink in my hands is her order.
5. I think _____ shoes on my feet are yours!

数量詞：名詞の前に付け、その数や量を表します。

可算名詞の前に使う	不可算名詞の前に使う	可算と不可算の両方に使う
many, few, another	much, little	more, less, some, any, other

C 例にならい、下線で示した部分を適切な数量詞に訂正しましょう。

例 I have so **many** homework these days!
         much

1. Would you like another milk?

2. Amy wants to buy much jackets.

3. Can I give you an other pencil?

4. There are little cookies on the table.

5. Tom has to buy five many textbooks.

Write to Speak

▶ 例にならい、必要があれば ____ に冠詞・指示詞・数量詞のいずれかを入れて、会話を完成させましょう。B は自分のことを答え、____ には適する語句を入れましょう。完成後、パートナーと会話練習をしましょう。

例 A: Did you eat *much* breakfast today?
   B: Yes, I ate *much*. / No, I ate *little*.

1. A: Do you live in _____ apartment?
   B: [Yes, I / No, I don't] live in _____ apartment.

2. A: Are there _____ students in this room?
   B: [Yes, there are _____ / No, there aren't _____] students.

3. A: Is _____ room cold?
   B: I think _____ room is _____.

4. A: Are _____ books on that counter yours?
   B: [Yes, _____ are / No, _____ _____] mine.

5. A: Are you from _____ London?
   B: No, I'm from _____ _____.

Word Power

▶ 例にならい、英文中の太字で示した部分を枠内の語句で書き換えましょう。

☐ apartment	☐ clothing	☐ dormitory
☐ looking forward to	☐ parents	☑ roommates

例 Three **people who share living space** live together.
　　　　roommates

1. Sarah still lives with her **mother and father**.

2. I am **happy about** the party tomorrow night.

3. Eric brought a lot of **jeans, shirts, and dresses** to his new house.

4. More than 50 students live in the **building where many students or workers live together**.

5. My **set of rooms inside a big building** has three bedrooms.

Listen Up!

A 会話を聞いて、問いに対する適切な解答を丸で囲みましょう。

1. Are Amy and David talking about a person? — [Yes, they are. / No, they aren't.]
2. Is their new roommate a guy or girl? — [A guy. / A girl.]
3. What is the new roommate's name? — [Melissa. / Dublin.]
4. Is the new roommate an Irish woman? — [Yes, she is. / No, she isn't.]
5. Who will share a room with the new roommate? — [David. / Amy.]
6. Does the new roommate have much clothing? — [Yes, she does. / No, she doesn't.]

UNIT 4 Life With A Roommate

B 音声を聞き、空所に枠内の語句を適切な形で入れて、会話を完成させましょう。ただし、2回使うものもあり、何も入れる必要がない場合は×を入れましょう。

☐ a	☐ an	☐ another	☐ apartment
☐ look forward to	☐ many	☐ much	☐ roommate
☐ that	☐ the	☐ this	

Amy: Hi David. I think I found ¹._____ ²._____ for ³._____ ⁴._____ .

David: Really? Is it ⁵._____ guy or girl?

Amy: Her name is Melissa. She comes from ⁶._____ Dublin.

David: Oh, is she ⁷._____ Irish woman?

Amy: Yes, she is. What do you think about ⁸._____ rooms?

David: Well, ⁹._____ room is mine, so ¹⁰._____ room can be yours and Melissa's.

Amy: OK. We can share ¹¹._____ room.

David: Does she have ¹²._____ things?

Amy: No, she doesn't have ¹³._____ books or ¹⁴._____ clothing.

David: That's good.

Amy: Yes, it is. I think she's ¹⁵._____ nice person.

David: I'm ¹⁶._____ meeting Melissa!

C パートナーと **B** の会話を読み合いましょう。

Ready to Read?

A 空所に枠内の単語を入れて、文章を完成させましょう。2回以上使うものもあります。何も入れる必要がない場合は×を入れましょう。

☐ a	☐ an	☐ apartment	☐ dormitory
☐ few	☐ many	☐ parents	☐ roommates
☐ that	☐ the	☐ those	

Three's Company

How do university students live in your country? Do they usually live at home with their 1._____? Do some people live in a dormitory? Do some students live in 2._____ apartment? The most usual way students live in North America is in an apartment with 3._____. This can be really fun, but it can also be very difficult.

The first place I lived when I was a student was 4._____ dormitory. The 5._____ had too many students. So, I moved into an 6._____ with my friend named Skippy. It was nice to live with another student in an apartment. I have very good memories from 7._____ time.

We sometimes cooked 8._____ dinner together. 9._____ dinner was never great, but we could have fun together. We also told each other many jokes and if 10._____ jokes were funny, we laughed so much! If we had some problems, we talked to each other about them. Those are 11._____ best memories I have about living with Skippy.

I also had a 12._____ problems living together with my friend. When I forgot to clean 13._____ kitchen, Skippy got angry at me. Sometimes he talked to [14.]_____ friend loudly the night before I had a test, so I got angry. Some of the problems we had were very funny. One time he looked at my feet and said, "[15.]_____ shoes are mine!" I looked down and saw that [16.]_____ shoes on my feet were Skippy's!

　　　　Living alone is easier than having [17.]_____ roommate in [18.]_____ ways. Having a roommate is sometimes difficult, but it's also great!

NOTES　usually「通常は」　usual「通常の」　laugh「笑う」　get angry at「…に怒る」
　　　　　loudly「大声で、うるさく」　alone「一人で」

B 次の英文が **A** の文章と合っていれば True を、合っていなければ False を丸で囲みましょう。

1. Most North American university students live in an apartment.　　[True / False]
2. The writer lived with one roommate in a dormitory.　　[True / False]
3. The writer never had a problem living with Skippy.　　[True / False]

C **A** の文章に関する質問の答えとして、最も適切なものを選びましょう。

1. Where is the second place the writer lived at university?
   (A) At home
   (B) In an apartment
   (C) In a dormitory

2. What did the writer do together with Skippy?
   (A) Cooked
   (B) Studied
   (C) Went shopping

3. Why did Skippy get angry at the writer?
   (A) He didn't clean the kitchen.
   (B) He talked too loudly.
   (C) He didn't study enough.

United Skills

 A 音声を聞きながら、次の文章を読みましょう。音声と異なる個所があるので、丸で囲みましょう（10個所）。

I have the very funny roommate from the Toronto. He really likes the music and he has much CDs. If he asks if the CD is mine, I always say, "No, those CD is yours!" He doesn't eat many food, so he is very thin. Last week he only ate a apple for each breakfast. I told him, "please eat all of this things on a table."

 B もう一度音声を聞いて、丸で囲んだ個所を訂正しましょう。

C 次の質問に対し、自分の答えを英語で書きましょう。

1. Have you ever shared a room or house? If so, with who? If not, do you want to do that?
   （ルームシェアをしたことはありますか。ある場合、誰とですか。ない場合は、そうしてみたいですか）

   _____
   _____

2. Which do you prefer, living alone, living with family, or living with friends? Why do you think so?
   （一人で暮らすことと、家族と暮らすこと、あるいは友達と暮らすことのどれが好きですか。その理由は何ですか）

   _____
   _____

D パートナーと交互に、**C** の質問と答えの発話練習をしましょう。

Unit 5
I'll Take A Vacation!
一般動詞

Grammar Insight

一般動詞は、人や動物などの動作を表します。用法によって、自動詞と他動詞に区別されます。

自動詞：目的語を必要としません。自動詞の直後に名詞が続くことはなく、名詞が必要な場合は前置詞を伴います。自動詞のあとの情報がなくても、文法的には正しい文となります。

> Michael **talks** *to his mother a lot*.
> I **ran** *every day last week*.
> Kate will **walk** *to work in the morning*.
> The train **arrived** *on time*.

A 例にならい、太字で示した自動詞のあとの情報を消しましょう。

例 I **sleep** ~~for more than eight hours every night~~.

1. Sandy will **look** at the painting in the museum.
2. The boy **cried** about his broken toy.
3. The book **fell** from Dave's desk.
4. I often **laugh** when talking to my friends.
5. The bus will **leave** for London at 4:45.

他動詞：必ず目的語を伴います。他動詞のあとの目的語がなければ、文法的に正しい文とは言えなくなります。

> He **likes** (suspense movies).　　　　Tina **raised** (her hand) during the class.
> She will **buy** (some gloves) tomorrow.　　I **carried** (the bag) to the car.

B 例にならい、太字で示した他動詞の目的語を（　）で囲み、なくても英文が文法的には正しいと言える情報があれば、それを消しましょう。

例　Patrick **has** (coffee) ~~every morning~~.

1. My father **teaches** French at a university.
2. Christopher **wanted** a new computer.
3. Carl will **ride** his bicycle over 500 kilometers this summer.
4. My mother **bakes** my favorite cookies whenever I go back home.
5. The child **broke** his favorite toy this afternoon.

注意したい他動詞：次の動詞の後ろには、前置詞をつけないようにしましょう。

他動詞		間違いやすい例
enter「…へ入る」	その建物に入る	○ enter the building × enter into the building
discuss「…について話し合う」	その問題について話し合う	○ discuss the problem × discuss about the problem
mention「…について（軽く）言う」	それについて軽くふれる	○ mention it × mention about it
marry「…と結婚する」	ケンと結婚する	○ marry Ken × marry with Ken
reach「…に着く」	駅に着く	○ reach the station × reach at the station
approach「…に接近する」	空港に近づく	○ approach the airport × approach to the airport
resemble「…に似ている」	彼の母親に似ている	○ resemble his mother × resemble with his mother
attend「…に出席する」	授業に出席する	○ attend the class × attend to the class
obey「…に従う」	彼女の助言に従う	○ obey her advice × obey with her advice
oppose「…に反対する」	彼の考えに反対する	○ oppose his idea × oppose to/against his idea

UNIT 5　I'll Take A Vacation!

C 例にならい、英文中の誤りを訂正しましょう。

例　I would like to mention ~~about~~ the problem with the system.

1. Mr. Smith attended to the meeting.
2. This fruit resembles with strawberry in flavor.
3. Ted married with Jane last Sunday.
4. He didn't approach to the front door.
5. Sarah wants to discuss about it with Martin.

Write to Speak

▶ 例にならい、空所に適する語句を入れたり応答を選んだりして、会話を完成させましょう。
Bは自分のことを答えましょう。完成後、パートナーと会話練習をしましょう。

例　A: What do you **want** for your next birthday?
　　B: I want *a new bike*.

1. A: What did you **do** last night?
   B: I _____.

2. A: Did you **buy** anything last week?
   B: I [bought / didn't buy] _____.

3. A: Where did you **eat** this morning?
   B: I ate at _____.

4. A: Do you **have** any plans for this Sunday?
   B: [Yes, I do. / No, I don't.]

5. A: Did you **walk** to school today?
   B: [Yes, I did. / No, I didn't.]

41

Word Power

▶ 例にならい、英文中の太字で示した部分を枠内の単語で書き換えましょう。必要があれば、適切な形にしましょう。

| ☐ cards | ☐ cheap | ☐ earn | ☐ envy |
| ☐ practice | ☑ shine | ☐ spend | ☐ sunblock |

例 The California sun **makes a strong light** almost every day in August.
　　　　　　　　　　　shines

1. I **want to be like** Kim because she is very good at speaking English.

2. Mike will **try again and again** baseball every day during summer vacation.

3. I often play **a game with thick paper** with my friends after school.

4. We can **get** some money by doing part-time jobs.

5. You should always put on **cream that stops sunshine** when you go to the beach.

6. Ramen is a very **low-cost** food for university students.

7. I will **use** about $25 at the store when I go shopping.

Listen Up!

 A 会話を聞いて、問いに対する適切な解答を丸で囲みましょう。

1. Are Daniel and Jessica going to the mountains? — [Yes, they are. / No, they aren't.]
2. Did Jessica sleep well last night? — [Yes, she did. / No, she didn't.]
3. Where will Jessica buy some cards? — [At a supermarket. / At a convenience store.]
4. Does the sun shine every day at the beach in July? — [Yes, it does. / No, it doesn't.]

UNIT 5 I'll Take A Vacation!

5. What did Daniel make? — [Some sunblock. / Some sandwiches.]

6. Who will carry Jessica's suitcase to the car? — [Daniel. / Jessica.]

B 太字で示した単語が他動詞の場合、その目的語を枠内から選んで空所に入れましょう。2 回使うものもあります。自動詞の場合は IV を入れましょう。

| ☐ a pack of cards | ☐ it | ☐ my clothes |
| ☐ some sandwiches | ☐ some sunblock | ☐ your suitcase |

Daniel: Jessica, are you almost ready for our trip to the beach?

Jessica: Of course, Daniel! I'm **putting** 1._____ into the suitcase now.

Daniel: Good. How did you **sleep** 2._____ last night?

Jessica: I slept very well last night so I'm ready. How do you **feel** 3._____?

Daniel: I feel great. Are you going to **bring** 4._____ to play at night?

Jessica: That's a good idea. I'll **buy** 5._____ at a convenience store on the way.

Daniel: OK. Let's **get** 6._____ at the store, too.

Jessica: Oh, right! I heard the sun **shines** 7._____ at the beach every day in July.

Daniel: I **made** 8._____ for us to eat on the way.

Jessica: Oh, thanks. I always like to **eat** some while traveling.

Daniel: Do you want me to **take** 9._____ to the car?

Jessica: No thanks. I'll **carry** 10._____.

C 音声を聞いて **B** の答えを確認しましょう。また、パートナーと **B** の会話を読み合いましょう。

Ready to Read?

A 文章中に太字で示した単語が他動詞の場合、（ ）に **TV** を入れ、その目的語に下線を引きましょう。自動詞の場合、（ ）に **IV** を入れましょう。

Summer Vacation!

How long is summer vacation in Japan? What do students usually do during this time? Some things about summer vacation are similar but some are different in the United States and Japan. First of all, summer vacation is during the hottest months of the year—June to August. Second, American students can **take** (1.   ) three months off from school! Do you **envy** (2.   ) them?

Some students just **relax** (3.   ) during summer vacation. They go back to their hometown and **meet** (4.   ) their family and old friends. But some students stay at school and study hard to **pass** (5.   ) classes that they had failed before. Other students take extra classes at summer school that are interesting to them. Some other students **practice** (6.   ) their favorite sports during summer vacation.

Of course, most American students **work** (7.   ) during summer vacation. Their parents don't **give** (8.   ) them much money, so they work at restaurants, movie theaters, and supermarkets. They **earn** (9.   ) money and **use** (10.   ) it to buy clothes, to spend time with friends, and to **take** (11.   ) trips. Working during summer vacation is a little hard, but most students like to work.

American university students also like to travel during summer vacation. They **drive** (12.   ) their own cars or **take** (13.   ) busses or trains to interesting places near or far from their home. Some students go on foreign trips to places like

Canada, Mexico, or even to Europe. They usually stay at cheap hotels and **spend** (14.   )
little money each day.

American summer vacations are long and students don't have to **study** (15.   )
during the hottest months of the year. American students **enjoy** (16.   ) themselves very
much during this time.

NOTES similar「似ている」 fail「落第する」 foreign「外国の」

B 次の英文が **A** の文章と合っていれば True を、合っていなければ False を丸で囲みましょう。

1. American summer vacation starts in August. [True / False]
2. American students get two months off for summer vacation. [True / False]
3. Some American students drive their own cars. [True / False]

C **A** の文章に関する質問の答えとして、最も適切なものを選びましょう。

1. Why do some American students take classes during summer?
   (A) Their parents want them to.
   (B) Classes are interesting.
   (C) Their teachers want them to.

2. Where do some American students work during summer vacation?
   (A) At a hotel
   (B) At a bakery
   (C) At a supermarket

3. What kind of hotels do American students usually stay at?
   (A) Expensive ones
   (B) Cheap ones
   (C) Dirty ones

United Skills

A 音声を聞きながら、次の文章を読みましょう。音声と異なる個所があるので、丸で囲みましょう (9個所)。

I like to go to hiking in the mountains every Saturday. I sometimes hike alone or I take with one of my friends. When I bring with a friend, we usually discuss about where we will go to hiking. Last time my friend mentioned about that he enjoyed to camping in the mountains. So, we prepared for everything for camping. We had to a really great time!

B もう一度音声を聞いて、丸で囲んだ個所を訂正しましょう。

C 次の質問に対し、自分の答えを英語で書きましょう。

1. What do you usually do during summer vacation? (夏休み中はいつも何をしますか)

2. Have you had a part-time job? If yes, what kind of job have you had? If not, what kind of job do you want to have?
   (アルバイトをしたことがありますか。ある場合、どんな仕事でしたか。ない場合、どんな仕事をしたいですか)

D パートナーと交互に、**C** の質問と答えの発話練習をしましょう。

Unit 6

How Is The Weather?
疑問文

Grammar Insight

〈be 動詞＋形容詞〉の **Yes/No** 疑問文：Unit 2 で学んだ be 動詞の Yes/No 疑問文を思い出しましょう。

be 動詞	主語	形容詞	例文：疑問文―応答
am	I	late	Am I late?—No, you **aren't**.
is	he / **she** / it	cold	Is she cold?—Yes, she **is**.
are	we / you / **they**	next	Are they next?—No, they **aren't**.

〈一般動詞＋形容詞〉の **Yes/No** 疑問文

do/does	主語	動詞＋形容詞	例文：疑問文―応答
do	I / we / you / they	**look** OK	Do I look OK?—Yes, you **do**.
does	he / she / **it**	**go** fast	Does it go fast?—No, it **doesn't**.

A 例にならい、空所に be 動詞または do/does を入れて、疑問文を完成させましょう。上の表も参考にしましょう。

例　*Do* they go to school on Saturdays?

1. _____ he like ice cream?

2. _____ you sad about the news?

3. _____ we need a ticket for the concert?

4. _____ it hot in this room?

5. _____ I taller than you?

wh 疑問文：who や what などの wh で始まる疑問詞を使った疑問文は、Yes/No 疑問文の先頭に wh 疑問詞を置きます。

wh 疑問詞	意味	wh 疑問詞	意味	wh 疑問詞	意味
what	何	where	どこ	why	なぜ
when	いつ	who	誰		

B 例にならい、空所に適切な wh 疑問詞を上の表から選んで入れ、疑問文を完成させましょう。同じものを 2 回使っても構いません。

例 *Why/When/Where* does Julie play soccer?

1. _____ are you so sad today?

2. _____ do you usually do your homework?

3. _____ do you usually eat for breakfast?

4. _____ is the post office?

5. _____ is your best friend?

how を使った疑問文：wh 疑問詞と同様に、how が文頭にきます。

よく使われるパターン	例文
How ＋ be 動詞＋主語	**How *is* your grandmother?**
How ＋形容詞＋ be 動詞＋主語 （fast / old / tall / big / far）	**How big *is* that box?**
How ＋ do/does ＋主語＋一般動詞の原形	**How *do* you study for a test?**
How often ＋ do/does ＋主語＋一般動詞の原形	**How often *does* he see his parents?**
How much ＋不可算名詞	**How much money *do* you have?**
How many ＋可算名詞の複数形（または複数を表す名詞）	**How many books *do* you have?**

UNIT 6 How Is The Weather?

C 例にならい、空所に適する単語を入れて、疑問文を完成させましょう。

例 How *many* people live in your house?

1. How _____ _____ Anthony go fishing?
2. How _____ you come to school every day?
3. How tall _____ your older sister?
4. How _____ meat _____ you want? *meat「肉」
5. How _____ your mother and father?

Write to Speak

▶ 例にならい、____ に適する単語を入れ、会話を完成させましょう。Bは自分のことを答え、____ には適する語句を入れましょう。完成後、パートナーと会話練習をしましょう。

例 A: *When* do you usually go to bed?
　　B: At about *twelve o'clock*.

1. A: _____ I the tallest student in our class?
   B: Yes, _____ _____. / No, _____ _____.

2. A: _____ _____ do you watch movies?
   B: About _____ time(s) a month / Never.

3. A: _____ you like to study English?
   B: Yes, I _____. / No, I _____.

4. A: _____ is your favorite actor?
   B: He's / She's _____.

5. A: _____ _____ brothers and sisters do you have?
   B: I have _____. / I _____ have any brothers and sisiters.

Word Power

▶ 例にならい、英文中の太字で示した部分を枠内の単語で書き換えましょう。

| ☐ agent | ☐ border | ☐ connected | ☐ desert |
| ☐ foreign | ☑ forest | ☐ somewhere | ☐ variety |

例 I love to walk in a **place with many trees**.
　　　　　　　　　　　　　forest

1. Danny wants to go **to a place he hasn't decided** for summer vacation.

2. Sarah lives in a **different** country now.

3. Sam talked to his travel **person who helps buy something** about his vacation.

4. The Sahara is the biggest **place that has very little rain** in the world.

5. Japan doesn't have a **line between nations** with any other country.

6. That restaurant has a big **choice** of dishes.

7. My computer and printer are **together** by a wire.

Listen Up!

A 会話を聞いて、問いに対する適切な解答を丸で囲みましょう。

1. Is the man a travel agent? — [Yes, he is. / No, he isn't.]
2. Does the woman want to go to a foreign country? — [Yes, she does. / No, she doesn't.]
3. Does the woman want to go somewhere cool? — [Yes, she does. / No, she doesn't.]
4. Is it dry in Bali in February? — [Yes, it is. / No, it isn't.]
5. How does the woman feel about Fiji's weather in February?
   — [It's very nice. / It's very rainy.]
6. Where will the woman probably go? — [To Bali. / To Fiji.]

B 空所に枠内の単語を適切な形で入れて、会話を完成させましょう。2回以上使うものもあります。

- agent
- are
- can
- do
- does
- foreign
- how
- is
- it
- somewhere
- what
- when
- where
- you

Man: Hello. I will be your travel 1._____ today. 2._____ _____ I help you today?

Woman: I want to go to a 3._____ country.

Man: OK. 4._____ _____ you want to go?

Woman: I want to go 5._____ warm. 6._____ _____ know a good place?

Man: Yes. 7._____ _____ you think about Bali?

Woman: It sounds nice. But 8._____ _____ rain a lot?

Man: Sometimes. 9._____ _____ you want to go?

Woman: I want to go in February. 10._____ _____ the weather that month?

Man: Oh, it rains a lot then. 11._____ _____ interested in Fiji?

Woman: Yes, I am. 12._____ warm 13._____ Fiji in February?

Man: It's usually warm, dry and sunny in February. 14._____ _____ you think?

Woman: It sounds very good to me.

C 音声を聞いて **B** の答えを確認しましょう。また、パートナーと **B** の会話を読み合いましょう。

Ready to Read?

A 空所に枠内の単語を適切な形で入れて、文章を完成させましょう。2回以上使うものもあります。

☐ big	☐ border	☐ connected	☐ desert
☐ does	☐ forest	☐ how	☐ is
☐ it	☐ sunny	☐ variety	☐ yes

California Dreaming 🎧 18

1._____ _____ the weather in your birthplace? Is it often 2._____? Does it rain a lot? I'm from a famous state in the U.S.A. called California. You have probably heard about its nice weather, but do you know what California's other weather is like?

First of all, California is a very big state. 3._____ _____ _____ it? Well, Japan is about 378,000 km², but California is even bigger at about 424,000 km². California's shape is also long, like Japan's. How long is it? Its top part is as far north as Hokkaido and its bottom 4._____ is as far south as Kyushu. 5._____ such a long state have different weather? Sure, it does!

There is also a lot of 6._____ in California's land. Does it have a lot of mountains like Japan? Yes, 7._____ _____. It also has many beaches, 8._____, and 9._____. In fact, the highest point (Whitney Mountain) and the lowest point (Death Valley) in the 10._____ 48 states are

both in California. ¹¹·_____ _____ get cold on Whitney Mountain? It sometimes becomes −25°C in winter! How hot is Death Valley? It once became 56.7°C in Death Valley and it was the hottest day in human history!

¹²·_____ all of California's weather so cold and hot? No, it isn't. Most of California's weather is warm, dry, and sunny especially near the sea. Is it the weather that we often see in movies? ¹³·_____, _____ _____! Movies are usually filmed in the south and near the sea.

NOTES state「州」 shape「形」 bottom「下部、底」

B 次の英文が **A** の文章と合っていれば True を、合っていなければ False を丸で囲みましょう。

1. Japan is bigger than California. [True / False]
2. Parts of California have very strong weather. [True / False]
3. All California weather is always very hot or cold. [True / False]

C **A** の文章に関する質問の答えとして、最も適切なものを選びましょう。

1. How big is California?
   (A) 378,000 km²
   (B) 324,000 km²
   (C) 424,000 km²

2. What does the writer say that Whitney Mountain and Death Valley in California have?
   (A) The highest and lowest points
   (B) The coldest and driest days
   (C) The sunniest and hottest days

3. Where is the California weather seen in movies?
   (A) Near the mountains in the south
   (B) Near the sea and in the south
   (C) Close to the deserts

United Skills

A 音声を聞きながら、次の文章を読みましょう。音声と異なる個所があるので、丸で囲みましょう（6個所）。

Where kind of weather do you like best? Does she like hot summer days? When does you feel on cold winter days? Some people love warm, sunny days. Some other people really like cool, rainy days. How are the type of person that likes these kinds of days? Or am I the kind of person that likes something different? Who kind of person are you?

B もう一度音声を聞いて、丸で囲んだ個所を訂正しましょう。

C 次の質問に対し、自分の答えを英語で書きましょう。

1. What kind of weather do you like best? （どのような天気がいちばん好きですか）

_____

_____

2. Which country do you want to visit? Why? （どの国に行きたいですか。その理由は何ですか）

_____

_____

D パートナーと交互に、**C** の質問と答えの発話練習をしましょう。

Unit 7
Did You Do The Dishes?
過去時制

Grammar Insight

be 動詞の過去形

主語	be 動詞	例文	
I / he / she / it	was	She **was** happy today.	**Was** she happy today?
we / you / they	were	They **were** here this morning.	**Were** they here this morning?

A 例にならい、空所に be 動詞の過去形を入れて、英文を完成させましょう。

例 *Was* it cold last night?

1. Amy and Frank _____ at the meeting today.
2. _____ you tired after the test?
3. _____ it your last class this year?
4. I _____ the best player on the team.
5. Ken _____ the office manager last year.

規則的に変化する一般動詞の過去形

動詞の語尾	過去形の作り方	例
e	d を付ける	live → live**d**
子音 + y	y を i に変えて ed を付ける	try → tr**ied**
母音 + 子音（w や y は例外）	子音を2つ重ねて ed を付ける	stop → sto**pped**
母音 + w または y	ed を付ける	show → show**ed** delay → delay**ed**
上記のパターンに該当しない動詞		clean → clean**ed** fill → fill**ed**

B 例にならい、太字で示した動詞の過去形を訂正しましょう。

例 Sara **sharred** her dessert with Mike.
　　　shared

1. I **relyed** on my brother for help.

2. Tom and Samantha **marryed** last year.

3. I **droped** my sister off at the station.

4. She **playd** the trumpet in high school.

5. They **studyed** all night for the test.

不規則に変化する一般動詞の過去形

have と do	母音が変化する動詞	完全に変わる動詞	変化しない動詞
have – h**a**d do – d**i**d	get – g**o**t sit – s**a**t drink – dr**a**nk	catch – caught bring – brought teach – taught	cut – cut hit – hit fit – fit

C 例にならい、太字で示した動詞や do が過去形であるかどうかを確認し、必要があれば訂正しましょう。

例 Pam **find** some money yesterday.
　　　found

1. **Do** you go home late last night?

2. We **eat** dinner at 7:00 p.m.

3. I **ride** a horse during my summer vacation.

4. My teacher **let** me take the test again.

5. Bob **send** Cathy a nice e-mail last week.

Write to Speak

▶ 例にならい、太字で示した動詞や do が過去形であるかどうかを確認し、必要があれば訂正しましょう。1と2のBは自分のことを答えましょう。完成後、パートナーと会話練習をしましょう。

例 A: ~~Do~~ you ride a bus to school today?
     Did
B: Yes, I ~~ride~~ a bus. / No, I ~~do not~~ ride a bus.
       rode   *didn't*

1. A: **Are** you happy yesterday?

   B: [Yes / No], I [**was** / **wasn't**] happy yesterday.

2. A: I **study** for _____ hour(s) last night. How about you?

   B: I **study** for _____ hour(s) last night.

3. A: **Do** you bring a pen to class today?

   B: Yes, I **bring** a pen to class.

4. A: **Do** you put your book on the table?

   B: Yes, I **put** my book on the table.

5. A: **Do** you sit on a chair yesterday?

   B: Yes, I **sit** on a chair yesterday.

Word Power

▶ 例にならい、英文中の太字で示した部分を枠内の語句で書き換えましょう。必要があれば、適切な形にしましょう。

| ☐ become | ☐ complain | ☐ dishwasher | ☐ fill |
| ☐ housework | ☐ sweep | ☐ vacuum | ☑ washing machine |

例 I have a big **machine to wash clothes**.
   washing machine

1. I want to **change myself to** a teacher in the future.

2. Joe **said something bad** about his dinner at the restaurant.

3. My roommate and I share all of the **cooking and cleaning**.

4. I need to buy a **machine to clean floors** soon.

5. Can you please **put something to the top of** my glass?

6. My mother asked me to **clean** the floors.

7. Cleaning the kitchen is easy if you have a good **machine to clean dishes**.

Listen Up!

 A 会話を聞いて、問いに対する適切な解答を丸で囲みましょう。

1. What are Angela and Scott talking about? — [Homework. / Housework.]
2. Did Scott fill the dishwasher? — [Yes, he did. / No, he didn't.]
3. Who turned on the dishwasher? — [Angela. / Scott.]
4. Did Scott turn on the washing machine? — [Yes, he did. / No, he didn't.]

5. Did Scott vacuum the floors? — [Yes, he did. / No, he didn't.]

6. Who swept the floors? — [Angela. / Scott.]

B 音声を聞き、空所に枠内の語句を適切な形で入れて、会話を完成させましょう。

☐ do	☐ dishwasher	☐ fill	☐ finish
☐ forget	☐ housework	☐ put	☐ sweep
☐ think	☐ turn	☐ vacuum	☐ washing machine

Angela: Scott, ¹._____ you finish the ²._____?

Scott: Hi Angela. Yes, I think I ³._____ everything.

Angela: Did you wash all of the dishes?

Scott: I ⁴._____ the ⁵._____ but I didn't turn it on yet.

Angela: That's OK. I ⁶._____ it on an hour ago.

Scott: I also ⁷._____ the clothes in the ⁸._____.

Angela: Did you remember to turn it on?

Scott: Uhh… No. I was on the phone, so I ⁹._____ to do that.

Angela: I ¹⁰._____ you might forget to do that.

Scott: Sorry. But I remembered to ¹¹._____ the carpets.

Angela: Great! How about the floors? Did you remember that?

Scott: Yes, I ¹²._____ the floors this morning!

C パートナーと **B** の会話を読み合いましょう。

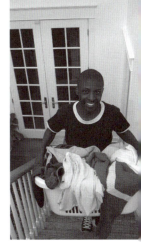

Ready to Read?

A （　）内の動詞を過去形に変えて、文章を完成させましょう。

Housework 🎧 21

Who did the housework when you (grow) ¹·_____ up? If you lived in a traditional home, your mother probably (do) ²·_____ most of the cooking and cleaning for the whole family. This (is) ³·_____ the usual situation in North America, but things have changed over the past 50 years.

5　　When I (am) ⁴·_____ very young, my mother did all of the housework. She was very busy at her job, but she came home and cooked and (clean) ⁵·_____ for everyone. She cooked us breakfast and dinner, (wash) ⁶·_____ our clothes and dishes, and (vacuum) ⁷·_____ the floors.

When my sister and I (become) ⁸·_____ a little bigger, she asked us to
10　help her do some of the housework. At first, we (take) ⁹·_____ the trash out and my father vacuumed the floors. This work was easy, but it helped my mother a lot. She could finally relax at home sometimes.

A few years later, my mother (ask) ¹⁰·_____ us to do more and more of the housework. We (start) ¹¹·_____ to wash the dishes and
15　clean the kitchen after every breakfast and dinner. We also washed our own clothes during the weekends and my father cooked dinner three times a week. We (be) ¹²·_____ very surprised to see him working in the kitchen!

A few more years later, we did most of the housework and
20　my mother could relax a lot. My sister and I even cooked dinner

once a week. We often (complain) ¹³._____ about doing the housework, but I'm very happy that she (make) ¹⁴._____ us do it. I could learn how to take care of myself.

NOTES traditional「伝統的な」 the whole family「家族全員」 vacuum「掃除機をかける」 trash「ごみ」
finally「ついに」 take care of myself「自己管理をする」

B 次の英文が **A** の文章と合っていれば True を、合っていなければ False を丸で囲みましょう。

1. The writer did all of the housework when she was very young.　[True / False]
2. The writer's father never did housework when she was very young.　[True / False]
3. North American mothers do less housework than before.　[True / False]

C **A** の文章に関する質問の答えとして、最も適切なものを選びましょう。

1. What housework did the writer and her sister do when they became a little bigger?
    (A) Cooked dinner
    (B) Took out the trash
    (C) Washed the dishes

2. How often did the writer's father cook dinner?
    (A) Every day
    (B) Three times a week
    (C) Once a week

3. Who often complained about doing the housework?
    (A) Mother
    (B) Father
    (C) Writer and her sister

United Skills

A 音声を聞きながら、次の文章を読みましょう。音声と異なる個所があるので、丸で囲みましょう（6個所）。

I really don't like to do the housework when I was younger. I really hate to take out the trash every day. My parents make me and my brother wash the dishes every night. We also have to vacuum the floors three times a week. But, I don't hated washing my clothes so much because it is nice to wear clean and fresh shirts.

B もう一度音声を聞いて、丸で囲んだ個所を訂正しましょう。

C 次の質問に対し、自分の答えを英語で書きましょう。

1. Who did the housework when you grew up? （あなたが小さかった頃、誰が家事をしていましたか）

2. Should family members share housework or should the mother mainly do housework? Why?
   （家族は家事を分担すべきですか、それとも母親が主に家事をすべきですか。その理由は何ですか）

D パートナーと交互に、**C**の質問と答えの発話練習をしましょう。

Unit 8

I'm Going To College
進行形

Grammar Insight

進行形：〈be 動詞＋動詞の ing 形〉で表します。

現在進行形：〈am/is/are ＋動詞の ing 形〉で「～している」という意味を表します。

種類	現在形	現在進行形
肯定文	Sharon **eats** fruit often.	Sharon **is eating** fruit now.
否定文	Sharon **doesn't eat** fruit often.	Sharon **isn't eating** fruit now.
疑問文	**Does** Sharon **eat** fruit often?	**Is** Sharon **eating** fruit now?

◎**実現性の高い予定**：現在進行形は「（近いうちに確実に）～する」という意味合いで、確定的な未来のことを表すことがあります。

　　He **is calling** to me in five minutes.

A 例にならい、空所に適する語句を入れて、英文を現在形または現在進行形にしましょう。必要があれば、（ ）内の動詞を適切な形にしましょう。

例　Be quiet! The baby (sleep) *is sleeping*.

1. _____ Melissa usually (ride) _____ her bicycle to school?

2. You don't need your umbrella because it (rain) _____.
3. Gary never (finish) _____ work early.
4. Laura (exercise) _____ almost every day.
5. _____ Frank (attend) _____ a class now?

過去進行形:〈was/were ＋動詞の ing 形〉で「〜していた」という意味を表します。

種類	過去形	過去進行形
肯定文	Neil **studied** history.	Neil **was studying** history for a year.
否定文	Neil **didn't study** history.	Neil **wasn't studying** history last year.
疑問文	**Did** Neil **study** history?	**Was** Neil **studying** history at that time?

B 例にならい、空所に適する語句を入れて、英文を過去形または過去進行形にしましょう。必要があれば、（　）内の動詞を適切な形にしましょう。

例　Joe (call) *called* me when I (take) *was taking* a bath.

1. _____ you (sleep) _____ when I came into the room?
2. Joe (cook) _____ for his family every day last week.
3. Roger never (visit) _____ his uncle in Alberta.
4. Did Martha come while you (do) _____ your homework?
5. Donna (cut) _____ her finger when she (cook) _____ dinner.

未来進行形:〈will ＋ be 動詞＋動詞の ing 形〉で「(特定のある未来に) 〜することになっている、〜することになるだろう」という意味を表します。

種類	未来形	未来進行形
肯定文	Frances **will stay** in Amy's room.	Frances **will be staying** in Amy's room until this evening.
否定文	Frances **won't stay** in Amy's room.	Frances **won't be staying** in Amy's room until this evening.
疑問文	**Will** Frances **stay** in Amy's room?	**Will** Frances **be staying** in Amy's room until this evening?

UNIT 8　I'm Going To College

C 例にならい、空所に適する語句を入れて、英文を未来形または未来進行形にしましょう。必要があれば、（　）内の動詞を適切な形にしましょう。

例　Carl (wait) *will be waiting* for us when our bus arrives.

1. _____ you still (cook) _____ while I clean the house?
2. Julie won't (visit) _____ any of her relatives while staying in San Diego.
3. Arthur (speak) _____ first at the meeting.
4. _____ you (attend) _____ the party tonight?
5. Eric said he (come) _____ late to the party.

Write to Speak

▶ 例にならい、空所に適する語句を入れ、会話を完成させましょう。必要があれば、（　）内の動詞を適切な形にしましょう。Bは自分のことを答えましょう。完成後、パートナーと会話練習をしましょう。

例　A: *Are* you (stand) *standing* now?
　　B: [Yes, I am / (No, I'm not)] (stand) *standing*.

1. A: _____ you (study) _____ English at nine last night?
   B: [Yes, I was / No, I wasn't] (study) _____ it.
2. A: _____ you (sleep) _____ at this time tomorrow?
   B: [Yes, I will / No, I won't] (sleep) _____.
3. A: _____ you (have) _____ fun now?
   B: [Yes, I am / No, I'm not] (have) _____ fun now.
4. A: _____ you (walk) _____ to school around 8:00 a.m. this morning?
   B: [Yes, I was / No, I wasn't] (walk) _____.
5. A: _____ you (work) _____ at midnight tonight?
   B: [Yes, I will / No, I won't] (work) _____.

Word Power

▶ 例にならい、英文中の太字で示した部分を枠内の語句で書き換えましょう。

☐ arrive ☐ cost ☐ double ☐ part-time job
☑ pay ☐ serious ☐ tuition ☐ worried

例 Carl will **give money** for my dinner tonight.
　　　　　　pay

1. Rent in New York is **two times** that of Dallas.

2. Our teacher was **not funny** today.

3. Mike will pay his university **money for school** by himself.

4. Linda is often **not relaxed** about taking a big test.

5. I am doing a **few hours of work a week** while going to university.

6. We will **reach** home at 8:00.

7. The **money needed** for a new car is going down.

Listen Up!

 **A** 会話を聞いて、問いに対する適切な解答を丸で囲みましょう。

1. Are Melissa and Thomas having a school party?
   — [Yes, they are. / No, they aren't.]
2. Is Melissa shopping now? — [Yes, she is. / No, she isn't.]
3. Is Melissa buying some drinks? — [Yes, she is. / No, she isn't.]
4. Did Melissa buy drinks yesterday? — [Yes, she did. / No, she didn't.]

UNIT 8　I'm Going To College

5. Is Thomas almost finished cleaning? — [Yes, he is. / No, he isn't.]

6. Are the guests arriving now? — [Yes, they are. / No, they aren't.]

B 音声を聞き、空所に枠内の語句を適切な形で入れて、会話を完成させましょう。2回使うものもあります。

| ☐ are | ☐ arrive | ☐ buy | ☐ clean | ☐ come | ☐ get |
| ☐ guest | ☐ I'm | ☐ look for | ☐ shop | ☐ worry | |

Melissa: Thomas, ¹·_____ you ²·_____ the house ready for our party tonight?

Thomas: Of course, Melissa. ³·_____ ⁴·_____ the living room right now.

Melissa: Oh, good. I'm ⁵·_____ at the supermarket now.

Thomas: Are you ⁶·_____ home soon?

Melissa: ⁷·_____ coming home right after shopping.

Thomas: I see. Are you ⁸·_____ some drinks?

Melissa: No, I ⁹·_____ them yesterday.

Thomas: OK. What ¹⁰·_____ you shopping for now?

Melissa: I'm ¹¹·_____ some chips and dip.

Thomas: Sounds good. I'm almost finished cleaning. I'm going to relax now.

Melissa: Is that OK? I'm ¹²·_____ that the house won't be ready.

Thomas: Don't worry! The ¹³·_____ aren't ¹⁴·_____ yet.

C パートナーと **B** の会話を読み合いましょう。

Ready to Read?

A 空所に適切な be 動詞や枠内の語句を入れて、文章を完成させましょう。（　）内の動詞は進行形に変えましょう。

☐ costs   ☐ double   ☐ part-time job   ☐ serious   ☐ tuition

Making My Way

Are you (go) ¹._____ to a university now? Who ²._____ paying your ³._____? Are you working at a ⁴._____? In Japan, parents usually pay their children's tuition, but students usually pay their own living ⁵._____ and education in North America. This has many merits, but it also has some bad points.

Students learn many important things about life when they pay their own living costs. For example, if they ⁶._____ paying their apartment rent, their food, and their gas, electricity, and water, they can learn how to use money carefully. They learn important lessons by doing this. I was working at a part-time job and I was (pay) ⁷._____ my own living costs when I was a university student. This was difficult, but I learned many important things about life at that time.

If students are paying their own education costs, they will be more ⁸._____ about school and study harder. But if their parents are paying, they might not study so hard. Many North American students ⁹._____ getting education money from a bank. They are (borrow) ¹⁰._____ the money now,

UNIT 8   I'm Going To College

and will ¹¹._____ paying it back in the future. But they might pay the money back for many, many years. This is because North American university tuition is almost ¹²._____ Japanese university tuition these days! I was lucky to finish university a long time ago. I ¹³._____ (pay) ¹⁴._____ my bank back for only five years.

   When students pay their own living and education costs, they are learning important lessons. But they ¹⁵._____ also paying the money back for a long, long time.

NOTES merit「長所、利点」 lessons「知識」 borrow「借りる」

B 次の英文が **A** の文章と合っていれば True を、合っていなければ False を丸で囲みましょう。

1. North American parents usually pay students' tuition. [True / False]
2. Students learn important lessons by paying living costs. [True / False]
3. Most North American students do not borrow money from a bank. [True / False]

C **A** の文章に関する質問の答えとして、最も適切なものを選びましょう。

1. What lessons do North American students learn by paying their own living costs?
   (A) How to study for an important test
   (B) How to cook and clean for themselves
   (C) How to use money carefully

2. How will students be if they are paying their own education costs?
   (A) More serious
   (B) Happier
   (C) More relaxed

3. How much does education cost in North America?
   (A) Two times Japan's
   (B) Half of Japan's
   (C) The same as Japan's

United Skills

A 音声を聞きながら、次の文章を読みましょう。音声と異なる個所があるので、丸で囲みましょう（9個所）。

I'm a student and I'm go to a university in Chicago. I'll taking five classes this semester and I going to each class two times a week. I'm also work three days a week at a part-time job. My parents are pay half of my rent and I'm pay the other half now. I was be graduate and look for a full-time job.

B もう一度音声を聞いて、丸で囲んだ個所を訂正しましょう。

C 次の質問に対し、自分の答えを英語で書きましょう。

1. Who is paying your tuition?（あなたの授業料を払っているのは誰ですか）

2. Are you doing or not doing a part-time job? Why or why not?
   （あなたはアルバイトをしていますか、それともしていませんか。その理由は何ですか）

D パートナーと交互に、**C** の質問と答えの発話練習をしましょう。

Unit 9 Have You Ever Had A Job?

現在完了

Grammar Insight

現在完了：〈have/has ＋過去分詞〉で表し、過去のことで現在に続いている場合などに使います。具体的な「時」を表す語句（yesterday や last week など）とともには使えません。

種類	例文	
肯定文	I **have worked** in a café.	She **has worked** in a café.
否定文	I **have not worked** in a café.	She **has not worked** in a café.
疑問文	**Have** you **worked** in a café?	**Has** she **worked** in a café?

A 空所に適する過去分詞を入れて、次の表を完成させましょう。

	原形	過去形	過去分詞
不規則動詞	be	was / were	been
	do	did	done
	have	had	1.
	find	found	2.
	fly	flew	3.
	hold	held	4.
	show	showed	5.
	ride	rode	6.
	take	took	7.

規則動詞	live	lived	lived
	try	tried	tried
	tap	tapped	**8.**
	fill	filled	**9.**
	knit	knitted	**10.**

B 例にならい、（　）内の動詞を過去分詞に変えて、現在完了の文を完成させましょう。

例　Ken **has** (take) *taken* the computer course.

1. They **have** (fill) _____ the kid's swimming pool.
2. The family **has** (ride) _____ a bus to Sacramento.
3. **Have** you (do) _____ your homework?
4. My boss **has** (show) _____ me the report.
5. Mike **has** (have) _____ a big dinner.

C 例にならい、（　）内の動詞を過去分詞に変えて、現在完了の文を完成させましょう。また、青色の「時」を表す語句のうち、現在完了の文には使わないものを消しましょう。

例　I **have** (fly) *flown* to Hong Kong ~~last year~~.

1. **Have** you (be) _____ to Bali before?
2. Bob **has** (take) _____ his kids to the beach five times last month.
3. Amy **has** (try) _____ surfing on Sunday.
4. She **hasn't** (find) _____ her books yet.
5. Carol and Sandra **have** (hold) _____ a koala in Australia in April.

Write to Speak

▶ 例にならい、（　）内の動詞を過去分詞に変えて空所に入れ、会話を完成させましょう。Bは自分のことを答えましょう。完成後、パートナーと会話練習をしましょう。

例　A: **Have** you ever (be) *been* to Sapporo?
　　B: [(Yes, I **have**.) / No, I **haven't**.]

1. A: **Has** your friend (fly) _____ to Paris?
　　B: [Yes, he/she **has**. / No, he/she **hasn't**.]

UNIT 9 Have You Ever Had A Job?

2. A: **Have** you ever (hold) _____ a rabbit?

   B: [Yes, I **have**. / No, I **haven't**.]

3. A: **Has** your teacher (live) _____ in Canada before?

   B: [Yes, he/she **has**. / No, he/she **hasn't**.]

4. A: **Have** you (buy) _____ a book recently?

   B: [Yes, I **have**. / No, I **haven't**.]

5. A: **Have** you (show) _____ your homework to your teacher?

   B: [Yes, I **have**. / No, I **haven't**.]

Word Power

▶ 例にならい、英文中の太字で示した部分を枠内の語句で書き換えましょう。

| ☐ apply for | ☐ company | ☐ experience | ☐ graduate |
| ☐ job hunting | ☑ job interview | ☐ résumé | |

例 John had a ~~meeting to get work~~ yesterday.
            job interview

1. Ken is working at a clothing **business**.

2. Laura will **finish going to school** in May.

3. I will start **looking for work** after I graduate from university.

4. You should bring your **paper showing your work history** to the job interview.

5. Please tell me about your work **history of doing something**.

6. She will **try to get** a job at a big company in Tokyo.

73

Listen Up!

A 会話を聞いて、問いに対する適切な解答を丸で囲みましょう。

1. Is Ms. Taylor at a television interview? — [Yes, she is. / No, she isn't.]

2. Has Ms. Taylor worked at a restaurant before? — [Yes, she has. / No, she hasn't.]

3. How long has Ms. Taylor kept her restaurant job? — [One year. / Two years.]

4. Has Ms. Taylor had experience cooking American food?
   — [Yes, she has. / No, she hasn't.]

5. Has Ms. Taylor eaten at their restaurant before?
   — [Yes, she has. / No, she hasn't.]

6. Has Ms. Taylor written her résumé yet? — [Yes, she has. / No, she hasn't.]

B 空所に枠内の語句や（　）内の動詞を適切な形に変えて入れ、会話を完成させましょう。

| ☐ apply for | ☐ experience | ☐ job interview | ☐ résumé |

Interviewer: Thank you for ¹·_____ this job, Ms. Taylor.

Ms. Taylor: Thank you very much for this ²·_____.

Interviewer: Have you (work) ³·_____ at a restaurant before?

Ms. Taylor: Yes. I have worked at the Sakura Japanese restaurant.

Interviewer: OK. How long have you (do) ⁴·_____ the Sakura restaurant job?

Ms. Taylor: I have done it for two years.

Interviewer: Have you ever (have) ⁵·_____ ⁶·_____ cooking American food?

Ms. Taylor: No. I have never (cook) ⁷·_____ American food before.

Interviewer: I see. Have you ever (eat) ⁸·_____ the food at our restaurant?

Ms. Taylor: Yes. I have eaten here three times before. I think it's great!

Interviewer: Oh, thank you. Have you written your ⁹·_____ yet?

Ms. Taylor: Yes. I (write) ¹⁰·_____ it last night. Here it is.

C 音声を聞いて **B** の答えを確認しましょう。また、パートナーと **B** の会話を読み合いましょう。

Ready to Read?

A 空所に枠内の語句や（ ）内の動詞の過去分詞を入れて、文章を完成させましょう。

☐ company   ☐ graduate   ☐ interviews   ☐ job hunting

Job Hunting

When do Japanese university students start ¹._____? It seems to happen earlier every year. Recently Japanese students even go to ²._____ during their third year of university. Job hunting is very different in North America. We usually take many classes until the end of our fourth year and start job hunting after we ³._____.

I have already (graduate) ⁴._____ from university and I have started job hunting. However, I haven't (find) ⁵._____ a job yet. I graduated in May and started job hunting very soon after that in June. I studied business during four years at my university. I would like to work at an international business in Los Angeles or New York.

I have (apply) ⁶._____ for work at a big international bank in New York. I sent them my résumé in June. I have already had two interviews with this ⁷._____. I have (have) ⁸._____ one interview in English and I have had one interview in Japanese. I will have one more interview next month.

I have also applied for a job at a car company in Los Angeles. I sent my résumé to this company last week. I have not (hear) ⁹._____ from them yet, but I hope to get an answer soon. I would love to have an interview with this company because I like cars so much.

20   I have (send) ¹⁰·_____ my résumé to many other companies, but the bank in New York and the car business in Los Angeles are the two I want most. I hope that I can find a good job soon!

....

B 次の英文が **A** の文章と合っていれば True を、合っていなければ False を丸で囲みましょう。

1. Japanese university students recently start job hunting after they graduate.
[True / False]

2. North American university students usually take many classes during their fourth year.
[True / False]

3. North American university students usually start job hunting during their third year.
[True / False]

C **A** の文章に関する質問の答えとして、最も適切なものを選びましょう。

1. When did the writer start job hunting?
   (A) June
   (B) May
   (C) Last week

2. How many interviews has the writer had with the international bank?
   (A) One
   (B) Two
   (C) Three

3. What does the writer hope to get from the car company in Los Angeles?
   (A) A car
   (B) A résumé
   (C) An answer

United Skills

A 音声を聞きながら、次の文章を読みましょう。音声と異なる個所があるので、丸で囲みましょう（8個所）。

I have being a university student for three years. I have have three part-time jobs. I have work in a restaurant kitchen. I have cooked hamburgers there until 2015. I have also sell clothes in a department store. I have enjoyed that job very much. I have working in a bookstore for a year, too. I have enjoy all three of these part-time jobs very much.

B もう一度音声を聞いて、丸で囲んだ個所を訂正しましょう。

C 次の質問に対し、自分の答えを英語で書きましょう。

1. Have you ever had a job interview? If so, what were you asked? If not, please imagine what would be asked in an interview.
   （仕事の面接試験を受けたことがありますか。ある場合、何を聞かれましたか。ない場合、何を聞かれるか想像しましょう）

   _____
   _____

2. What do you want to do in the future? （将来あなたは何をしたいですか）

   _____
   _____

D パートナーと交互に、**C** の質問と答えの発話練習をしましょう。

Unit 10 She Had Been Great!

過去完了

Grammar Insight

過去完了：〈had ＋過去分詞〉で、過去のある時点まで続いていた、過去のことを表す場合に使います。

種類	例文
肯定文	Paul **had lived** in a small town before he got the prize.
否定文	Paul **had not lived** in a big city before he got the prize.
疑問文	**Had** Paul **lived** in a small town before he got the prize?

A 空所に適する過去分詞を入れて、次の表を完成させましょう。

	原形	過去形	過去分詞
不規則動詞	drive	drove	driven
	drink	drank	drunk
	cut	cut	**1.**
	come	came	**2.**
	eat	ate	**3.**
	give	gave	**4.**
	go	went	**5.**
	see	saw	**6.**
	win	won	**7.**

規則動詞	agree	agreed	agreed
	study	studied	studied
	admit	admitted	**8.**
	bake	baked	**9.**
	move	moved	**10.**

B 例にならい、英文を 2 つの部分（時間）に分けましょう。また、（ ） 内の動詞を過去分詞に変えて空所に入れ、過去完了の文を完成させましょう。

例　The boy **had** (drink) *drunk* all of his milk **/** before he went to sleep.

1. Terry **had** (drive) _____ to Chicago five times before she took a train.
2. **Had** Brian (eat) _____ lunch before he saw the movie?
3. Anna **had** (lose) _____ her bag, so she couldn't pay for her dinner.
4. She **had not** (live) _____ in California long before she met Thomas.
5. By the time he died, Frank **had** (give) _____ all of his money to the poor.

過去完了進行形：〈had ＋ been ＋動詞の ing 形〉で表します。

種類	例文
肯定文	Karen **had been playing** a game when her mother arrived.
否定文	Karen **had not been playing** a game when her mother arrived.
疑問文	**Had** Karen **been playing** a game when her mother arrived?

C 例にならい、英文を 2 つの部分（時間）に分けましょう。また、（ ） 内の動詞を ing 形に変えて空所に入れ、過去完了進行形の文を完成させましょう。

例　Rebecca **had been** (talk) *talking* to Joe **/** when the train arrived.

1. I **had been** (watch) _____ the news on TV when someone came to my door.
2. **Had** you **been** (wait) _____ long before the store opened?
3. The team **had been** (win) _____ the game when it started to rain.
4. Carol **had not been** (sleep) _____ long when Mike woke her up.
5. Tim really wanted to sit down since he **had been** (stand) _____ all day at work.

UNIT 10 She Had Been Great!

Write to Speak

▶ 例にならい、（　）内の動詞を適切な形に変えて空所に入れ、会話を完成させましょう。B は自分のことを答えましょう。完成後、パートナーと会話練習をしましょう。

例 A: **Had** you (study) *studied* English long before taking this class?

B: [Yes, I **had**. / No, I **hadn't**.]

1. A: **Had** you (do) _____ homework before going to bed last night?

   B: [Yes, I **had**. / No, I **hadn't**.]

2. A: **Had** your teacher (be) _____ in this room by the time you arrived?

   B: [Yes, he/she **had**. / No, he/she **hadn't**.]

3. A: **Had** you **been** (talk) _____ to your friend when this class started?

   B: [Yes, I **had**. / No, I **hadn't**.]

4. A: **Had** you **been** (sit) _____ at a table while eating today's breakfast?

   B: [Yes, I **had**. / No, I **hadn't**.]

5. A: **Had** your teacher **been** (write) _____ something when you came into the room?

   B: [Yes, he/she **had**. / No, he/she **hadn't**.]

Word Power

▶ 例にならい、英文中の太字で示した部分を枠内の語句で書き換えましょう。

☐ athlete ☐ award ☐ congratulations
☐ outside ☐ pass ☑ successful

例 Elizabeth Martinez is a very **good and famous** musician.
　　　　　　　　　　　　　　　　　　　　successful

1. **Words to tell someone when they are successful** for getting a new job!

2. Bobby had been good at sports, so he became a professional **sports player**.

3. Ms. Baker got a special **prize, present, medal, etc.** for her wonderful painting.

4. Sam studied very hard to **be successful at taking** his math test.

5. Janet's children love to play **outdoors** in the summer.

Listen Up!

A 会話を聞いて、次の問いに対する適切な解答を丸で囲みましょう。

1. Has Mr. Adams been chosen for an award? — [Yes, he has. / No, he hasn't.]
2. Had Mr. Adams been walking to work? — [Yes, he had. / No, he hadn't.]
3. Had Mr. Adams seen a house fire before? — [Yes, he had. / No, he hadn't.]
4. Had a baby been in the burning house? — [Yes, it had. / No, it hadn't.]
5. Had Mr. Adams won an award before? — [Yes, he had. / No, he hadn't.]
6. Had Mr. Adams run into a burning house before? — [Yes, he had. / No, he hadn't.]

B 空所に枠内の単語や（ ）内の動詞のing形または過去分詞を入れて、会話を完成させましょう。必要があれば、適切な形にしましょう。

☐ award   ☐ congratulations   ☐ happen   ☐ outside

Reporter: You have been chosen for the Good Citizen [1.]_____.
[2.]_____!

Mr. Adams: Thank you very much.

Reporter: Can you please tell us about the fire, Mr. Adams?

Mr. Adams: Sure. I had been (drive) [3.]_____ to work when I saw the house on fire.

Reporter: I see. Had you ever (see) [4.]_____ a fire before that one?

Mr. Adams: No, I hadn't.

Reporter: OK. What [5.]_____ next?

Mr. Adams: I had just (get) [6.]_____ out of my car when I heard that a baby was in the house.

Reporter: Oh, my gosh! What had you been (think) [7.]_____ before you ran into the house?

Mr. Adams: I had only (think) [8.]_____ about the baby. So, I ran in and took the baby [9.]_____.

Reporter: That's great! Had you ever (win) [10.]_____ an award before winning this one?

Mr. Adams: No, I hadn't. I had never (run) [11.]_____ into a burning house, either!

 C 音声を聞いて **B** の答えを確認しましょう。また、パートナーと **B** の会話を読み合いましょう。

Ready to Read?

A 空所に枠内の単語や（　）内の動詞を必要に応じて適切な形にして入れて、文章を完成させましょう。

☐ athlete ☐ award ☐ pass ☐ successful

My Amazing Friend

Do you have a friend who was very 1._____ in high school? Did he or she win any 2._____? I had many high school friends who studied hard or played sports well. Some of them were successful at taking tests or playing sports. However, one of my friends named Sandra was very successful at everything she tried
5 during high school.

Sandra had been good at studying before she became a great student in high school. She had 3._____ all of her tests during her first year when she became a second-year student. Unfortunately, she never got a perfect score. She (study) 4._____ very hard during her second year and got 100 percent on a test for the
10 first time. By her third year, she had (get) 5._____ 100 percent on every test she took. Sandra had (become) 6._____ a really great student when she became a third-year student. In fact, she won the Best Student of the Year award.

While she (study) 7._____ so hard, Sandra also played on the high school soccer team.
15 She practiced very hard and tried her best during games. Her coach (choose) 8._____ her to be a forward for her team. She was a great forward. She even scored five goals when she

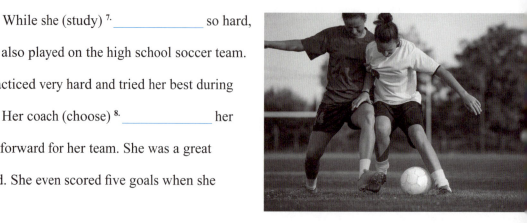

UNIT 10 She Had Been Great!

(be) 9._____ (play) 10._____ a game! Sandra was a great student and a great 11._____, too. She even won the Best Athlete award in addition to Best Student.

I had (know) 12._____ Sandra for three years when I graduated from high school. She had been a good friend and she had (make) 13._____ a great impression on me by the time we graduated.

NOTES during「…の間」 forward「フォワード（サッカーやバスケットボールなどのポジション）」
impression「印象」

B 次の英文が **A** の文章と合っていれば True を、合っていなければ False を丸で囲みましょう。

1. The story is about someone who had been successful in college. [True / False]
2. Sandra had won two awards during high school. [True / False]
3. Sandra had made a bad impression on the writer. [True / False]

C **A** の文章に関する質問の答えとして、最も適切なものを選びましょう。

1. How many times had Sandra gotten 100 percent during her first year at high school?
   (A) Two times
   (B) Never
   (C) Three times

2. How many goals had Sandra scored during a soccer match?
   (A) Five
   (B) Four
   (C) Three

3. How long had the writer known Sandra during high school?
   (A) One year
   (B) Two years
   (C) Three years

United Skills

 A 音声を聞きながら、次の文章を読みましょう。音声と異なる個所があるので、丸で囲みましょう（6個所）。

Jane had getting an award when she was in high school. She had swimming since she was only three years old. She had be a good swimmer when she been in middle school, but she has practicing very hard after she entered high school. Jane had been win an Olympic gold medal in swimming when she was only 17 years old.

 B もう一度音声を聞いて、丸で囲んだ個所を訂正しましょう。

C 次の質問に対し、自分の答えを英語で書きましょう。

1. Had you ever won an award before you became a high-school student? If so, what was it?（高校生になる前に、賞を受けたことがありますか。ある場合、それは何ですか）

___

___

2. Had you studied very hard before you graduated from high school? Why or why not?（高校を卒業する前、一生懸命勉強しましたか。その理由は何ですか）

___

___

D パートナーと交互に、**C** の質問と答えの発話練習をしましょう。

Unit 11 How Is Christmas Celebrated?

受動態

Grammar Insight

受動態：〈be 動詞＋過去分詞〉で「〜される」という意味になります。

時制	能動態	受動態
現在	*Jack* **cleans** the house.	The house **is cleaned** by *Jack*.
過去	*Pamela* **bought** the food.	The food **was bought** by *Pamela*.
未来	*Amy* **will finish** the work tomorrow.	The work **will be finished** by *Amy* tomorrow.

A 例にならい、時制（太字）に注意しながら、英文を受動態に変えましょう。

例 Mary **ate** the cookies.

→ The cookies *were eaten* by *Mary*.

1. Peter **will cook** dinner tomorrow.

    → Dinner _____ by _____ tomorrow.

2. She usually **cleans** the house.

    → The house _____ by _____.

3. Robert **will wash** the dishes.

    → The dishes _____ by _____.

4. They **gave** the present to Marty.

   → The present _____ to Marty by _____.

5. A foreign visitor **asked** a question.

   → A question _____ by _____.

進行形の受動態：〈be 動詞＋being＋過去分詞〉で「まさに〜されているところである」という意味合いになります。

時制	能動態	受動態
現在	*Eric* **is painting** a picture.	A picture **is being painted** by *Eric*.
過去	*A teacher* **was helping** Nancy.	Nancy **was being helped** by *a teacher*.

B 例にならい、時制（太字）に注意しながら、英文を受動態に変えましょう。

例　Susan **is pouring** drinks.

　　→ Drinks *are being poured* by *Susan*.

1. We **are buying** a house.

   → A house _____ by _____.

2. Carl **was selling** his car.

   → A car _____ by _____.

3. She **was writing** a book.

   → A book _____ by _____.

4. Lisa **is calling** them.

   → They _____ by _____.

5. We **were helping** him.

   → He _____ by _____.

完了形の受動態：〈have/has または had＋been＋過去分詞〉で「〜されていた」という意味合いになります。

時制	能動態	受動態
現在完了	*The students* **have visited** that museum.	That museum **has been visited** by *the students*.
過去完了	*Gloria* **had cleaned** her house before the party.	The house **had been cleaned** by *Gloria* before the party.

UNIT 11　How Is Christmas Celebrated?

C 例にならい、時制（太字）に注意しながら、英文を受動態に変えましょう。

例　Laura **has taken** the medicine.
→ The medicine *has been taken* by *Laura*.

1. They **have repaired** the bicycles.
   → The bicycles _____ by _____.

2. Carol **had bought** tickets before the game.
   → Tickets _____ by _____ before the game.

3. I **have told** the students five times.
   → The students _____ five times by _____.

4. Jason **has cut** the grass.
   → The grass _____ by _____.

5. The boys **had walked** the dog before school.
   → The dog _____ by _____ before school.

Write to Speak

▶ 例にならい、空所に適する語句や受動態を入れて、会話を完成させましょう。B は自分のことを答えましょう。完成後、パートナーと会話練習をしましょう。

例　A: Do you clean your own room?
　　B: [(Yes.) / No.] My room *is cleaned* by *me*.

1. A: Has your teacher given you homework?
   B: [Yes. / No.] I _____ homework by _____.

2. A: Were these students studying English yesterday?
   B: [Yes. / No.] English _____ by _____ yesterday.

3. A: Did you buy your own textbook?
   B: [Yes. / No.] My textbook _____ bought by _____.

4. A: Will the teacher teach this class tomorrow?
   B: [Yes. / No.] This class _____
      by _____ tomorrow.

5. A: Am I holding your book?
   B: [Yes. / No.] My book _____
      by _____ .

Word Power

▶ 例にならい、英文中の太字で示した部分を枠内の単語で書き換えましょう。必要があれば、適切な形にしましょう。

☐ aunt   ☐ couple   ☐ cousin   ☐ custom   ☐ decorate   ☑ pretty

例 Pie is a ~~very~~ sweet Christmas dessert.
       pretty

1. Giving presents is a nice Christmas **usual thing to do**.

2. My **mother's sister** lives in New York City.

3. Many **pairs of people** go on dates for Christmas in Japan.

4. Our house is **made more beautiful** each Christmas.

5. I will visit my **mother's sister's child** this summer vacation.

Listen Up!

🎧 A 会話を聞いて、次の問いに対する適切な解答を丸で囲みましょう。

1. Are they talking about a birthday party? — [Yes, they are. / No, they aren't.]

2. Who will join the party? — [Family members. / Friends.]

3. Was the house cleaned by James' cousins? — [Yes, it was. / No, it wasn't.]

UNIT 1   How Is Christmas Celebrated?

4. Is a chicken being cooked by someone? — [Yes, it is. / No, it isn't.]
5. Who has cooked the turkey for the past five years? — [Dianna. / James' aunt.]
6. Who was the pumpkin pie bought by? — [Mike. / James.]

B 音声を聞き、枠内の単語や（ ）内の動詞を変えたり受動態にしたりして空所に入れ、会話を完成させましょう。必要があれば、適切な形にしましょう。

☐ aunt   ☐ cousin   ☐ pretty

Dianna: James, how is our family Christmas dinner going?

James: ¹._____ good, Dianna. The food (buy) ²._____ by my mother on Tuesday.

Dianna: Good. Was the house (clean) ³._____ by someone?

James: Yes. It (be) ⁴._____ usually (clean) ⁵._____ by my mother every year.

Dianna: Who cleaned it this year?

James: It (clean) ⁶._____ by my ⁷._____ yesterday.

Dianna: That's nice. How about the turkey?

James: It (cook) ⁸._____ by my ⁹._____ right now.

Dianna: Has she cooked a turkey before?

James: Sure! The turkey (cook) ¹⁰._____ by my aunt for the past five years.

Dianna: How about the pumpkin pie?

James: Oh, it (buy) ¹¹._____ by Mike at a supermarket.

C パートナーと **B** の会話を読み合いましょう。

Ready to Read?

A 空所に枠内の単語や（　）内の動詞の受動態または過去分詞を入れて、文章を完成させましょう。必要があれば、適切な形にしましょう。

☐ couple　　☐ cousin　　☐ decorate　　☐ ring

Christmas Customs

Christmas is (celebrate) 1._____ differently in each part of the world. How is Christmas celebrated in Japan? Is fried chicken (eat) 2._____ by everybody? (Be) 3._____ presents given to family and friends? Do young 4._____ go out on dates? Of course Europe, Japan, and other nations have unique

5　Christmas customs, but it is celebrated uniquely in North America, too.

First of all, Christmas (enjoy) 5._____ by families in North America like the New Year holiday is celebrated in Japan. I remember the best Christmas Day that I have ever had. The tree was 6._____ two weeks before Christmas Day by me, my parents, my brother, and my sister. The smell of pine was wonderful. Presents

10　(buy) 7._____ by all of us and they (put) 8._____ under the tree during the days before Christmas Day.

The house is usually cleaned by my mother, but I, my brother, and my sister cleaned it for her that

15　year. A turkey (put) 9._____ into the oven by my mother on that Christmas morning. We cleaned the house while the turkey (cook) 10._____. There was a wonderful smell of turkey and Christmas tree in the house.

We (visit) **11.** _____ by most of our **12.** _____ every year except David. He had been living in Europe for ten years and never came home for Christmas. But, that year was different. While we were all talking in the living room, the doorbell was **13.** _____ by someone. I opened it and David was there! It was a big surprise. We were all happy, but my grandmother was the happiest to (visit) **14.** _____ by David.

NOTES celebrate「祝う」 unique「独特な」 except「…以外、…を除いて」 doorbell「玄関の呼び鈴」

B 次の英文が **A** の文章と合っていれば True を、合っていなければ False を丸で囲みましょう。

1. The story is mainly about Christmas in North America.　　[True / False]
2. North American Christmas is the same as in Japan.　　[True / False]
3. North American Christmas is mainly for families.　　[True / False]

C **A** の文章に関する質問の答えとして、最も適切なものを選びましょう。

1. When were presents put under the Christmas tree?
    (A) Before Christmas Day
    (B) On Christmas morning
    (C) On Christmas night

2. Who put the turkey in the oven?
    (A) The writer's brother and sister
    (B) The writer's cousin
    (C) The writer's mother

3. Who visited the writer's family?
    (A) Santa Claus
    (B) A friend
    (C) David

United Skills

 A 音声を聞きながら、次の文章を読みましょう。音声と異なる個所があるので、丸で囲みましょう（6個所）。

Christmas is celebrating by my family every year. Each time, the tree was decorated by children. Funny stories are told by my grandfather in the living room while dinner had been cooked by my mother. Presents will be bought by my family in the days before Christmas. These presents had been given to everybody after dinner. Christmas is being celebrated by my family since I was born.

 B もう一度音声を聞いて、丸で囲んだ個所を訂正しましょう。

C 次の質問に対し、自分の答えを英語で書きましょう。

1. What are you called by your friends and family members?
   （あなたは、友達や家族から何と呼ばれていますか）

   _____

   _____

2. What is your most memorable present? Why?
   （いちばん記憶に残っているプレゼントは何ですか。その理由は何ですか）

   _____

   _____

D パートナーと交互に、**C** の質問と答えの発話練習をしましょう。

Unit 12 Do You Want To Take Some Time Off?

不定詞

Grammar Insight

不定詞の名詞用法：不定詞は〈to ＋動詞の原形〉で、名詞句の役割をするものがあります。これらは「〜すること」と訳すことができます。

> He helped **to cook** dinner.
>
> **To play** with fire is very dangerous.
>
> Nicholas wants **to enjoy** his life more.
>
> **To eat** too fast is not healthy.

A 例にならい、英文中の不定詞（句）に下線を引き、意味の切れ目にスラッシュを入れましょう。

例 Mark likes **/** to play the guitar.

1. I promise to meet you at two o'clock.
2. Please remember to give me a call tomorrow.
3. To fail at something is a chance of learning.
4. They agreed to buy a new car.
5. To help a friend is a wonderful thing.

不定詞の形容詞用法：名詞を説明します。「〜するための」と訳すことができ、通常は直前の名詞を修飾します。

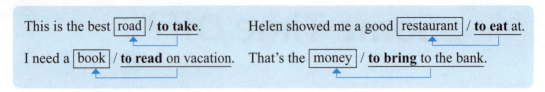

B 例にならい、英文中の不定詞（句）に下線を引き、その直前にスラッシュを入れましょう。また、その不定詞が修飾する名詞を丸で囲みましょう。

例 These are the (papers) / to give to Ryan.

1. Your idea to finish early sounds good.
2. Scott's promise to do his homework was broken.
3. The company's plan to open another store is foolish.
4. Your advice to come early was good.
5. The way to go to San Jose isn't easy.

不定詞の副詞用法：原因や理由を述べ、「〜するために」「〜して」と訳すことができます。また、動詞を修飾します。

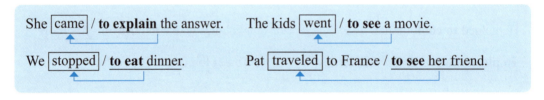

C 例にならい、英文中の不定詞（句）に下線を引き、その直前にスラッシュを入れましょう。また、その不定詞が修飾する動詞（句）を丸で囲みましょう。

例 Beth (made a plan) / to start a new business.

1. The boss had a meeting to talk to his workers.
2. James stopped to see the roses.
3. Mary exercises at the gym to stay healthy.
4. She called to tell us the bad news.
5. We will go to Arizona to see our grandparents.

UNIT 12 Do You Want To Take Some Time Off?

原形不定詞：助動詞 can/could, may/might, must, should, will/would や、動詞 feel, hear, let, make, see, watch に続く場合、to 不定詞の to が省略されます。

> Sheila might ~~to~~ **eat** early tonight.   You could ~~to~~ **stay** at my house tonight.
>
> Bruce watched his friend ~~to~~ **bake** a cake.   My mother let me ~~to~~ **go** to the game.

D 例にならい、英文中の助動詞または動詞を丸で囲み、不定詞（句）に下線を引きましょう。また、不要な to を消しましょう。

例 He (should) ~~to~~ go home early.

1. I watched my friend to play baseball on Sunday.
2. Amy will to study more for her test.
3. Tom makes his kids to go to bed early every night.
4. You can to start the test now.
5. She saw Jason to cross the street.

Write to Speak

▶ 例にならい、空所を埋めて自由に質問を作り、会話を完成させましょう。B は自分のことを答えましょう。完成後、パートナーと会話練習をしましょう。

例 A: Can you *play the piano*?
    B: [Yes, I can. / No, I can't.]

1. A: Did you go to a restaurant to _____?
   B: [Yes, I did. / No, I didn't.]

2. A: Is this a good time to _____?
   B: [Yes, it is. / No, it isn't.]

3. A: Do you want your father or mother to _____?
   B: [Yes, I do. / No, I don't.]

4. A: Should I _____?
   B: [Yes, you should. / No, you shouldn't.]

5. A: Did you ask a friend to _____?
   B: [Yes, I did. / No, I didn't.]

Word Power

▶ 例にならい、英文中の太字で示した部分を枠内の語句で書き換えましょう。必要があれば、適切な形にしましょう。

| ☐ do volunteer work | ☐ foreign language | ☐ normal |
| ☐ poor | ☑ semester | ☐ take some time off |

例 I go to school for two **half a year of going to school** every year.
　　　　　　　　　　　　　　　semesters

1. My sister went to Laos to work for people who are **needing help**.

2. She **worked for no money** to help people learn math.

3. Amy can speak three **ways of speaking in other countries**.

4. It is very **usual** to take your shoes off when you go into a Japanese house.

5. Stan is tired so he will **stop doing something to rest**.

Listen Up!

 A 会話を聞いて、問いに対する適切な解答を丸で囲みましょう。

1. Are Susan and Charlie teachers? — [Yes, they are. / No, they aren't.]
2. Is Susan tired from studying? — [Yes, she is. / No, she isn't.]
3. Did Susan tell Charlie to take some time off? — [Yes, she did. / No, she didn't.]
4. Does Susan have a plan to go to Asia? — [Yes, she does. / No, she doesn't.]
5. Did Susan ask her parents to let her travel? — [Yes, she did. / No, she didn't.]
6. Did Susan ask Charlie if he wanted to join her? — [Yes, she did. / No, she didn't.]

UNIT 12 Do You Want To Take Some Time Off?

B 空所に枠内の語句や（ ）内の動詞を適切な形にして入れて、会話を完成させましょう。

☐ semester   ☐ take some time off

Charlie: How are you, Susan?

Susan: Hi Charlie. I'm really tired from studying so hard.

Charlie: Maybe you should ¹·_____.

Susan: Yes. I hope (take) ²·_____ next ³·_____ off.

Charlie: What do you want (do) ⁴·_____ ?

Susan: I want (go) ⁵·_____ to Europe to see friends and travel.

Charlie: Will your parents let you (do) ⁶·_____ that?

Susan: Yes. I already asked them (let) ⁷·_____ me go to Europe.

Charlie: That's nice. I would love (go) ⁸·_____ with you.

Susan: Do you want (join) ⁹·_____ me?

Charlie: That sounds like a great idea.

Susan: OK. Let's make some plans (go) ¹⁰·_____ together!

C 音声を聞いて **B** の答えを確認しましょう。また、パートナーと **B** の会話を読み合いましょう。

Ready to Read?

A 空所に枠内の語句や（ ）内の動詞を適切な形にして入れて、文章を完成させましょう。

- ☐ do volunteer work
- ☐ foreign language
- ☐ normal
- ☐ poor
- ☐ semester

Taking Time Off

How long have you been a student? Are you tired of studying? Do you sometimes feel that you want (take) 1._____ some time off? This is a very normal feeling for students in Japan and every other part of the world. Students in some nations normally take a year off after high school (relax) 2._____, travel, or 3._____
5 before they start college. This is not 4._____ in North America yet, but many students take at least one 5._____ off during their college years.

I took one semester off during college. I wanted (enjoy) 6._____ many experiences and learn many things about life that I couldn't learn from books. I decided (travel) 7._____ around Europe for a few months. I took this trip
10 (see) 8._____ some friends and practice a 9._____. I also traveled around to see many different cultures of Europe. This was a wonderful trip that changed my life!

Some students take a semester off (become) 10._____ a volunteer. One of my friends
15 went to Cambodia (do) 11._____ volunteer work. He went (teach) 12._____ English to children in 13._____ parts of Cambodia. He also helped to teach math and science to

100

young Cambodians. He thought that poor children should (learn) ¹⁴._____ many important things. He told me that this time off from studying changed his life, too!

More and more, students are taking time off from studying (travel) ¹⁵._____ or do volunteer work. They can learn many things that schools can't teach them. Do you think you might (take) ¹⁶._____ some time off during your college years?

NOTES be tired of 「…に疲れる、飽きる」 practice 「練習する」

B 次の英文が **A** の文章と合っていれば True を、合っていなければ False を丸で囲みましょう。

1. American students normally take a year off after high school. [True / False]
2. The writer took one semester off to travel. [True / False]
3. The writer's friend took time off to do volunteer work. [True / False]

C **A** の文章に関する質問の答えとして、最も適切なものを選びましょう。

1. Why did the writer go to Europe?
   (A) To do volunteer work
   (B) To teach a foreign language
   (C) To have many experiences

2. What did the writer's friend do in Cambodia?
   (A) Practiced a foreign language
   (B) Taught English to poor children
   (C) Met many of his volunteer friends

3. What is good about taking time off from studying?
   (A) Students can learn something that schools don't teach them.
   (B) Students can start studying for their next classes.
   (C) Students can start looking for a good job in a foreign country.

United Skills

A 音声を聞きながら、次の文章を読みましょう。音声と異なる個所があるので、丸で囲みましょう（5個所）。

I have been studying hard for many years, so I want take some time off. Two years ago, I came to the university study business. My father said I should to graduate soon and find a job. But yesterday, I went to a travel agency talk about traveling in Asia for two months. I hope my father will let me to go.

B もう一度音声を聞いて、丸で囲んだ個所を訂正しましょう。

C 次の質問に対し、自分の答えを英語で書きましょう。

1. What do you like to do when you can take a lot of time off?
   （休暇をたっぷり取れたら、何をしたいですか）

   _____

   _____

2. Why did you choose this school? （なぜこの学校を選んだのですか）

   _____

   _____

D パートナーと交互に、**C** の質問と答えの発話練習をしましょう。

Unit 13 I Can Drive!
助動詞 can, will

Grammar Insight

can：動詞の前に置いて、「〜できる」「〜してもよい」などの意味を表します。

用法	例文
能力（できる／できない）	Ann **can**/**can't** speak Spanish.
許可（してもよい）	**Can** *I* sit down here?
依頼（してくれる）	**Can** *you* help me?
可能性（するかもしれない）	The meeting **can** be long.

A 例にならい、空所に can または can't を入れて、英文を完成させましょう。必要があれば、適切な形にしましょう。また上の表を参考にして、can の用法を書きましょう。

例 *Can* you help me cook dinner? ［用法］ 依頼

1. Steve _____ play the piano but he can play the guitar. ［用法］ _____
2. _____ the guests come to the party early? ［用法］ _____
3. She is a professional, so she _____ sing well. ［用法］ _____
4. _____ children play here? ［用法］ _____
5. _____ you help me with my homework? ［用法］ _____

103

will：「～するぞ」という強い意志や未来のことを表します。

用法	例文
意志（やる気がある／やる気がない）	I **will**/**won't (will not)** wash the dishes tonight.
未来	It **will** rain tomorrow.

B 例にならい、空所に will または won't を入れて、英文を完成させましょう。必要があれば適切な形にしましょう。また上の表を参考にして、will の用法を書きましょう。

例　I like cake so I *will* come to the party.　　　　　　　　　　　［用法］　意志

1. Because it's a nice day, the dog _____ come into the house.　　　　　　　　　　　［用法］_____

2. _____ tomorrow be a warm day?　　　　　　　　　　　［用法］_____

3. Susan wants to meet her family, so she _____ stay here all day.　　　　　　　　　　　［用法］_____

4. We _____ do our best to win the game.　　　　　　　　　　　［用法］_____

5. I think next year _____ be better than this year.　　　　　　　　　　　［用法］_____

C 例にならい、［　］内の用法に合うように、空所に can または will を適切な形で入れて、英文を完成させましょう。

例　［能力］　　I *can* speak English, so I will help you.

1. ［意志］　　I don't like singing, so I _____ come to sing karaoke.

2. ［依頼］　　_____ you help me clean the house?

3. ［可能性］　He is busy, so he _____ come to the park today.

4. ［意志］　　We _____ take our grandmother to dinner for her birthday.

5. ［未来］　　Laura thinks it _____ snow a lot this winter.

UNIT 13 I Can Drive!

Write to Speak

▶ 例にならい、空所に can または will を適切な形で入れて、会話を完成させましょう。B は自分のことを答えましょう。完成後、パートナーと会話練習をしましょう。

例 A: *Will* you eat cake today?
　　B: [Yes, I will. / No, I won't.]

1. A: _____ you play the violin?
   B: [Yes, I _____ . / No, I _____ .]

2. A: _____ it rain tomorrow?
   B: [Yes, it _____ . / No, it _____ .]

3. A: _____ you help me learn English?
   B: [Yes, I _____ . / No, I _____ .]

4. A: _____ our teacher give us homework?
   B: [Yes, he/she _____ . / No, he/she _____ .]

5. A: _____ your friend run fast?
   B: [Yes, he/she _____ . / No, he/she _____ .]

Word Power

▶ 例にならい、英文中の太字で示した部分を枠内の語句で書き換えましょう。必要があれば、適切な形にしましょう。

☐ danger	☐ education	☑ license
☐ motorcycle	☐ parking lot	☐ rule

例 You can't drive a car if you don't have a driver's **card that says you can do something**.
　　　　　　　　　　　　　　　　　　　　　　　　　　　　　　　license

1. I took a driver's **study** course at a driving school.

2. It is very important to follow driving **ways everyone should do something**.

3. My apartment has a very big **space to put cars in**.

4. You should never forget the **high risks** of driving too fast!

5. Many students ride **bicycles with engines** to school.

Listen Up!

 会話を聞いて、問いに対する適切な解答を丸で囲みましょう。

1. Can Chris drive a car yet? — [Yes, he can. / No, he can't.]
2. Can Sharon drive a car yet? — [Yes, she can. / No, she can't.]
3. Will Sharon go to the beach with her family? — [Yes, she will. / No, she won't.]
4. Who will drive a car to the beach? — [Chris. / Sharon's brother.]
5. Can Chris go to the beach on Sunday? — [Yes, he can. / No, he can't.]
6. When will they go to the beach? — [Saturday. / Sunday.]

UNIT 13 I Can Drive!

B 空所に枠内の語句を適切な形で入れて、会話を完成させましょう。2回以上使うものもあります。

| ☐ can ☐ can't ☐ driver's license ☐ will |

Sharon: Chris, ^{1.}_____ you drive a car yet?

Chris: Yes. I got my ^{2.}_____ last month. How about you, Sharon?

Sharon: Not yet. But I ^{3.}_____ try to get my license next month.

Chris: Sounds good. Why did you ask me?

Sharon: Well, I ^{4.}_____ go to the beach with some friends on Sunday.

Chris: I see. ^{5.}_____ I go with you?

Sharon: Sure! That's why I asked you about your driver's license.

Chris: Oh, do you want me to drive my mother's car?

Sharon: Yes. Can you do that for us?

Chris: I ^{6.}_____ drive on Sunday, but how about Saturday?

Sharon: I think Saturday is OK. ^{7.}_____ we leave at nine o'clock?

Chris: OK. I ^{8.}_____ come to your house by nine.

 C 音声を聞いて **B** の答えを確認しましょう。また、パートナーと **B** の会話を読み合いましょう。

Ready to Read?

A 空所に枠内の語句を入れて、文章を完成させましょう。必要があれば、適切な形にしましょう。2回以上使うものもあります。

☐ can	☐ danger	☐ motorcycle	☐ parking lot	☐ will
☐ driver's education course			☐ driver's training course	

I Can Drive!

1._____ you drive a car yet? Will you get a driver's license soon? In Japan, people 2._____ get a driver's license at 18 years old in all parts of the nation. The United States is different because each state decides its own rules. 3._____ you believe that young people can start driving in California on city roads at 15 ½ years old?

First, they must take a 4._____. In this course, they 5._____ learn the rules and laws of driving in California. They 6._____ also learn about the 7._____ of driving a car or 8._____. They 9._____ take this course at a driving school or they 10._____ take the course at their high school!

After they have taken the driver's education course, they 11._____ take a 12._____. During this course, they will start driving with a professional teacher. Can you believe that they will take their driver's training course on city roads, not a special training course like in Japan?

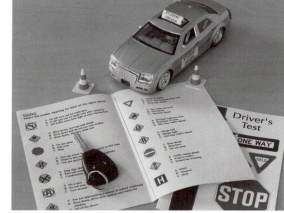

108

UNIT **13** I Can Drive!

If they ¹³·_____ pass their driver's training course, they can get a training license. They can drive with someone over 24 years old. They often drive with their older friend, their mother or father, or their brother or sister. When they are 16 years old, they ¹⁴·_____ take a paper test and a driving test. If they pass these tests, they ¹⁵·_____ get their license. Then they can drive as usual drivers.

After these young people get their driver's license, they ¹⁶·_____ usually drive a car to their high school. Can you believe that the students' ¹⁷·_____ is often much bigger than the teachers' and staff's parking lot?

NOTES law「法律」

B 次の英文が **A** の文章と合っていれば True を、合っていなければ False を丸で囲みましょう。

1. This story is about getting a driver's license in all American states. [True / False]
2. Each American state has its own driving rules. [True / False]
3. The teachers' and staff's parking lot is bigger than the students' at California high schools. [True / False]

C **A** の文章に関する質問の答えとして、最も適切なものを選びましょう。

1. What will people in California do first to get a driver's license?
   (A) Take a driver's training course.
   (B) Take a driver's education course.
   (C) Practice driving with someone over 24 years old.
2. Where do people in California take a driver's training course?
   (A) On city streets
   (B) On a special training course
   (C) In a high school
3. What is the earliest age that people in California can drive as usual drivers?
   (A) 15 ½   (B) 16   (C) 24

United Skills

 A 音声を聞きながら、次の文章を読みましょう。音声と異なる個所があるので、丸で囲みましょう（6個所）。

I'm 16 years old but I will drive a car already. My friend is not 16 yet so she can drive alone. I got my driver's license last month so I will drive alone. I won't drive my car to my high school tomorrow but I will park in the high school parking lot. I can't also drive to my part-time job tomorrow after school.

 B もう一度音声を聞いて、丸で囲んだ個所を訂正しましょう。

C 次の質問に対し、自分の答えを英語で書きましょう。

1. Can you drive a car? Why or why not? （車を運転できますか。その理由は何ですか）

   _____
   _____

2. Do you think your life will be better or not with a car? Why?
   （車があればあなたの生活はよくなると思いますか、あるいはよくなりませんか。その理由は何ですか）

   _____
   _____

D パートナーと交互に、**C** の質問と答えの発話練習をしましょう。

Unit 14 Where Would You Like To Go?

助動詞 could, would

Grammar Insight

could：can の過去形で、次のような用法があります。

用法	例文
丁寧な許可	**Could** *I* borrow your pen?
丁寧な依頼	**Could** *you* please sit down?
提案	We **could** go to the beach.
未来の可能性	It **could** rain tomorrow.

A 例にならい、空所に could を入れて、英文を完成させましょう。また上の表を参考にして、could の用法を書きましょう。

例　*Could* you wash the dishes, please?　　　　　　　［用法］　丁寧な依頼

1. We _____ study at the library tonight.　　　［用法］_____
2. _____ I please have another piece of cake?　［用法］_____
3. My friend Ken _____ join us tomorrow.　　　［用法］_____
4. _____ I come a little late?　　　　　　　　　［用法］_____
5. Susan Davis _____ be our next president.　　［用法］_____

would：will の過去形で、次のような用法の慣用表現があります。

用法	例文
丁寧な許可	**Would you mind if** we **ate** together?
丁寧な依頼	**Would you** pass the salt, **please**?
勧誘	**Would** you **like to** play golf tomorrow?
好み	**Would** you **like** tea **or** coffee?

B 例にならい、空所に would を使った慣用表現を入れて、英文を完成させましょう。（ ）内の動詞は適切な形にしましょう。また上の表を参考にして、would の用法を書きましょう。

例 _Would you mind if_ I (turn) _turned_ on the TV?　　　　［用法］__丁寧な許可__

1. _____ you _____ _____ go to San Diego with me?
   　　　　［用法］_____
2. _____ you please come here?　　　　［用法］_____
3. _____ you _____ chicken _____ beef?
   　　　　［用法］_____
4. _____ _____ _____ _____ I (eat)
   _____ before you?　　　　［用法］_____
5. _____ you _____ _____ join us?
   　　　　［用法］_____

C 例にならい、[ ] 内の用法に合うように、空所に could または would を使った慣用表現を入れて、英文を完成させましょう。（ ）内の動詞は適切な形にしましょう。

例 ［丁寧な依頼］　　_Could_ you please open the window?

1. ［丁寧な許可］　　_____ I join the meeting?
2. ［勧誘］　　_____ you _____ _____ come with us tomorrow?
3. ［丁寧な依頼］　　_____ you please be quiet?
4. ［好み］　　_____ your children _____ cake _____ ice cream?
5. ［未来の可能性］　It _____ snow a lot this winter.

UNIT 14 Where Would You Like To Go?

6. ［提案］　　　　We _____ take the fast train.

7. ［丁寧な許可］　_____ _____ _____ _____

　　　　　　　　I (bring) _____ a friend with me?

Write to Speak

▶ 例にならい、空所に could または would を使った慣用表現を適切な形で入れて、会話を完成させましょう。必ず B は自分のことを答えましょう。完成後、パートナーと会話練習をしましょう。

例　A: *Would* you *like to* eat cake today?

　　B: [Yes, I *would*. / No, I *wouldn't*.]

1. A: _____ you smile for me, please?

　　B: [Sure. / Sorry, but I can't.]

2. A: _____ you please give me 500 yen?

　　B: [Yes, I _____. / No, I _____.]

3. A: It _____ snow tonight!

　　B: [Yes, it _____. / No, it _____.]

4. A: _____ you _____ rice _____ bread with dinner?

　　B: [I _____ like rice. / I _____ like bread.]

5. A: _____ I sit next to you?

　　B: [Sure, go ahead. / Sorry, the seat is already taken.]

Word Power

▶ 例にならい、英文中の太字で示した部分を枠内の語句で書き換えましょう。必要があれば、適切な形にしましょう。

☐ decide	☑ difficult	☐ either
☐ join	☐ take a trip	☐ weekend

例 Driving all night is very **hard to do** and dangerous.
　　　　　　　　　　　　　　　　difficult

1. Could my brother **come together with** us for dinner?

2. Let's drive somewhere this **Saturday and Sunday**.

3. Sam **chose** to go to England this spring.

4. We could have **a choice of two things**, Italian or Chinese food tonight.

5. Will Amy **go somewhere** this summer vacation?

Listen Up!

A 会話を聞いて、問いに対する適切な解答を丸で囲みましょう。

1. Would Michael like to drive somewhere this weekend?
   — [Yes, he would. / No, he wouldn't.]

2. Where would Michael like to go? — [San Francisco. / Santa Barbara.]

3. Whose car would Michael like to take? — [Lisa's. / Michael's.]

4. Would Lisa like Kate to join them? — [Yes, she would. / No, she wouldn't.]

5. Would Michael like Jerry to join them? — [Yes, he would. / No, he wouldn't.]

6. Could it snow on Saturday? — [Yes, it could. / No, it couldn't.]

UNIT 14 *Where Would You Like To Go?*

B 音声を聞き、空所に枠内の語句を適切な形で入れて、会話を完成させましょう。2 回以上使うものもあります。

☐ ask   ☐ could   ☐ join   ☐ like to   ☐ or
☐ weekend   ☐ would   ☐ would like to   ☐ would you mind if

Lisa: Hi Michael. Would you like to drive somewhere this ¹._____?

Michael: Hi Lisa. Yes, I ²._____ do that.

Lisa: Great! Where ³._____ you ⁴._____ go?

Michael: We ⁵._____ drive to Santa Barbara.

Lisa: That sounds nice. Would you ⁶._____ take my car ⁷._____ your car?

Michael: ⁸._____ you drive your car?

Lisa: Sure. ⁹._____ I ¹⁰._____ Kate to ¹¹._____ us?

Michael: No problem. ¹²._____ I ask Jerry to come, too?

Lisa: Of course. It sounds fun!

Michael: Oh, it ¹³._____ rain on Saturday.

Lisa: Yes, I know. But it ¹⁴._____ be sunny, too!

Michael: That's true!

C パートナーと **B** の会話を読み合いましょう。

Ready to Read?

A 空所に枠内の語句を適切な形で入れて、文章を完成させましょう。2回以上使うものもあります。

☐ could ☐ decide ☐ difficult ☐ either ☐ like to
☐ take a trip ☐ would ☐ would like to ☐ would you mind if

Road Trip

1._____ you 2._____ drive your car to a far-away place with a friend? 3._____ it took two or three weeks? This type of traveling is called a "road trip" in North America. When I was 20 years old, my friend Nancy asked me to go on a big road trip with her.

We lived in California but we were both really interested in going to Florida. On the first day of summer vacation, Nancy asked me if I 4._____ 5._____ with her. She said that we could go there to try Florida's famous oranges and beaches. I thought it was a great idea!

Nancy said that the road trip to Florida and back to California 6._____ take three weeks or more. I told her that three weeks was OK. She also asked me if I 7._____ take my car or hers on the road trip across the United States. I said that we 8._____ take 9._____ car, but hers was newer than mine. After all, we 10._____ to take Nancy's car to Florida. Nancy asked me if I 11._____ drive first on the road trip. I told her that I could do that because I really liked driving.

UNIT 14 Where Would You Like To Go?

We planned our road trip very carefully and asked our parents if we
12. _____ drive to Florida. But, we decided that the trip would be too
13. _____ and too dangerous. We never went on our road trip, but we had a lot of
fun planning it!

NOTES famous「有名な」 across「…を横切って」

B 次の英文が **A** の文章と合っていれば True を、合っていなければ False を丸で囲みましょう。

1. The writer asked Nancy to go on a road trip. 　　　　[True / False]
2. The writer and Nancy lived in Florida. 　　　　　　　[True / False]
3. The writer and Nancy never went on their road trip. 　[True / False]

C **A** の文章に関する質問の答えとして、最も適切なものを選びましょう。

1. When did the writer plan to go on a road trip?
   (A) During summer vacation
   (B) When he or she lived in Florida
   (C) During spring vacation

2. Whose car did the writer and Nancy decide to take?
   (A) The writer's
   (B) Nancy's father's
   (C) Nancy's

3. Who was going to drive first on the road trip?
   (A) Nancy
   (B) Another friend
   (C) The writer

United Skills

A 音声を聞きながら、次の文章を読みましょう。音声と異なる個所があるので、丸で囲みましょう（9個所）。

Would you want to have dinner together tomorrow night? Could you mind if we go to an Italian restaurant? We would go to the new one near my house. Would you drive to my house first? Could you like to invite Joe and Betty to come with us? It would rain tomorrow night, so bring your umbrella! Could you please call me back soon?

B もう一度音声を聞いて、丸で囲んだ個所を訂正しましょう。

C 次の質問に対し、自分の答えを英語で書きましょう。

1. What would you like to eat for lunch? （昼食に何を食べたいですか）

_____

_____

2. If you were the Prime Minister, what would you like to do?
   （あなたが総理大臣だったら、何をしたいと思いますか）

_____

_____

D パートナーと交互に、**C** の質問と答えの発話練習をしましょう。

References

Unit 1
http://www.stvalentinesday.org/valentines-day-in-us.html
http://www.timeanddate.com/holidays/us/valentine-day

Unit 3
http://ushfc.org/about/#fancy-form-delay
http://www.npr.org/sections/thesalt/2011/12/31/144478009/the-average-american-ate-literally-a-ton-this-year
http://www.cdc.gov/nchs/data/databriefs/db114.htm
https://www.dosomething.org/facts/11-facts-about-american-eating-habits
http://www.cbsnews.com/news/americans-are-obsessed-with-fast-food-the-dark-side-of-the-all-american-meal/
http://www.niddk.nih.gov/health-information/health-statistics/Pages/overweight-obesity-statistics.aspx
http://www.huffingtonpost.com/2014/01/02/chicken-vs-beef_n_4525366.htm

Unit 5
http://www.marketwatch.com/story/nearly-4-out-of-5-students-work-2013-08-07

Unit 6
http://www.guinnessworldrecords.com/world-records/highest-recorded-temperature/
http://timberlinetrails.net/WhitneyWeather.html

Unit 7
http://edition.cnn.com/2013/04/08/opinion/york-equal-housework/
http://www.usatoday.com/story/news/nation/2013/03/14/men-women-work-time/1983271/

Unit 8
http://thisjapaneselife.org/2012/07/12/costs-of-education-japan/
http://atlasp.net/questions/88.html
http://www.wsj.com/articles/SB10001424052702304815004579417262095065046
http://www.top10onlinecolleges.org/college-tuition/

Unit 9
http://www.japantimes.co.jp/news/2015/09/15/national/keidanren-rethink-timing-annual-student-recruitment-drive/#.ViM90RArIQ8
http://univinjapan.com/shukatsu.html
http://www.careercast.com/career-news/job-hunting-college-grads-survival-guide

Unit 11
http://www.whychristmas.com/cultures/usa.shtml

Unit 13
https://www.dmv.ca.gov/portal/dmv/?1dmy&urile=wcm:path:/dmv_content_en/dmv/dl/dl_info#PERMINOR

Unit 14
http://www.roadtripamerica.com/

クラス用音声CD有り（別売）

English Insight
—An Integrated Approach to Language Learning
使いながら身につける基本文法総合演習

2016年3月1日　初版発行

著　者　Mark D. Stafford、妻鳥千鶴子、松井こずえ
発行者　松村達生
発行所　センゲージ ラーニング株式会社
　　　〒102-0073　東京都千代田区九段北1-11-11　第2フナトビル5階
　　　電話　03-3511-4392
　　　FAX　03-3511-4391
　　　e-mail: elt@cengagejapan.com
　　　copyright © 2016 センゲージ ラーニング株式会社

装　　丁　株式会社クリエーターズユニオン　森村直美
組　　版　有限会社ザイン
印刷・製本　株式会社平河工業社

ISBN 978-4-86312-280-2

もし落丁、乱丁、その他不良品がありましたら、お取り替えいたします。
本書の全部または一部を無断で複写（コピー）することは、著作権法上での例外を除き、禁じられていますのでご注意ください。